For Our Babies

For Our Babies

Ending the Invisible Neglect
of America's Infants

J. Ronald Lally

FOREWORD BY
T. Berry Brazelton
& Joshua Sparrow

 Teachers College
Columbia University
New York and London

WestEd.org

Published simultaneously by Teachers College Press, 1234 Amsterdam Avenue, New York, NY 10027, and WestEd, 730 Harrison Street, San Francisco, CA 94107.

Library of Congress Cataloging-in-Publication Data

Lally, J. Ronald (John Ronald)
    For our babies : ending the invisible neglect of America's infants / by J. Ronald
    Lally ; foreword by T. Berry Brazelton & Joshua Sparrow.
        pages cm
    Includes bibliographical references and index.
    ISBN 978-0-8077-5424-5 (pbk. : alk. paper)
        1. Child care workers—United States. 2. Infants—Care—United States. 3.
    Child care—United States. 4. Day care centers—United States. I. Title.
    HQ778.63.L35 2013
    362.70973—dc23   2012048329

ISBN 978-0-8077-5424-5 (paper)

Printed on acid-free paper
Manufactured in the United States of America

20   19   18   17   16   15   14   13   8   7   6   5   4   3   2   1

To Edward Zigler,
for his tireless support of young children

Contents

Foreword

It is not news that infants are born both highly competent and highly vulnerable. In the 1950s, I (TBB) began studying newborns and discovered through careful observation of their skin color, activity, neurological reflexes, sensory function, and social responsiveness that they indeed come into the world as highly competent beings, wired for human interaction that shapes their brains (Brazelton & Nugent, *Neonatal Behavioral Assessment Scale Manual*, 1st edition 1971, 4th edition 2011). Back then we didn't have the noninvasive brain imaging technologies of today, but our scientific methods were already revealing that far more was going on in infants' brains than was once thought.

Future scientific advances will no doubt reveal much more about the developing brain, and how crude our current understandings are. Yet for decades we've known enough to know that the workplace's increasing demands on families and the unraveling of informal neighborhood supports are incompatible with what babies need at the beginning of life to thrive later on.

It is also not news that babies shape their caregivers to be responsive to their unique, individual needs. For this, caregivers must be present, emotionally available, and protected from too many other demands. Otherwise, the critical signals babies send to their caregivers may go unheeded. The role of such exchanges in healthy infant and parent development was first established in the *Face-to-Face* experiments that I began with colleagues back in the 1970s. In the 1980s, I began to see in my pediatric practice the transformation of families, described in *For Our Babies*, that can jeopardize this kind of early communication. I wrote *Working and Caring* to address the challenges that families were facing as they found themselves with too little time for their young children and not enough support for themselves as parents. Since then, real wages stagnated and then declined, pushing parents to spend even more time at work and less with their children. To counter this, a few years later, I worked with Congressional leaders to bring about the Family Medical Leave Act. As Lally says, it hasn't increased the time parents actually spend with their babies because the leave is too short and unpaid.

With more parents in the workforce, and without paid parental leave, more babies are spending more time in childcare. Yet we've known for years that the majority of child care in this country is poor quality. Some small steps have been taken on this front in recent years. Despite the worst financial crisis since the Great Depression, the first Obama administration invested more money in quality early childhood education than has been invested at any time since the creation of Head Start more than 40 years ago. Yet most babies and young children still do not receive the quality of care that they need for success later in life.

These critical policy gaps in parental leave and quality early childhood education have been exacerbated by additional stresses on families, for example, the dissolution of extended families and communities by the relentlessly increasing requirements of the workplace, the contamination of family and neighborhood values by TV shows designed to make us pay more attention to things to buy than to each other in our vanishing free time, and the paving over of neighborhoods to accommodate cars rather than human connections. In 1991, I published the first book in my *Touchpoints* series on children's development—the predictable developmental crises that are major challenges for the whole family—because I saw that their successful resolution was being jeopardized by these gaps and stresses. These normal and necessary crises that ultimately propel growth are times when parents need the support of extended family, friends, and neighbors. With that support, temporary disorganization leads to reorganization at a higher level, with new skills and capacities for the child and parents. Without it, developmental derailment is a major risk. At that time, I thought the only solution was to help health care, educational, and other human service professionals to learn to fill in for the relationships in families that were being lost. Since then, I've realized that although this can help, it is not enough. We must instead reorient our priorities and our communities around families raising children.

In 2001, I wrote a book with the late Stanley Greenspan, *The Irreducible Needs of Children*, which was motivated by a mission similar to this book—to use science to inform new policies to address these gaps. But Ron Lally's book comes at a different time, a time when the trickle-down economics and deregulation culminating in the Great Recession of 2008 have increased the number of children living in poverty and stretched families' and communities' resources even further. With an historic federal deficit, effective programs for children and families are at risk of being cut back or dismantled altogether at a time when more children need them more than ever. This is a dire time, a touchpoint for our country through which we can grow and gather strength—or be derailed.

This book is an urgent call to action. In it, Lally decries the fact that the United States is the only wealthy, industrialized nation without paid parental leave and affordable, quality early education. For years, he and others have presented such comparisons with other countries in order to stimulate constructive debate and spur progress. Instead, the result has been knee-jerk responses about American exceptionalism: "Are you saying we're not the greatest? How dare you compare us with *those* countries?" As a result, the point is missed: The most successful businesses study the successes of their competitors and their own failures in order to make their products better than anyone's. We need to do the same with our policies. We can *expand* the exceptionalism of our great country, but we will need this crisis to push us to think differently, and then to act. Together.

For Our Babies proposes a science-based approach to policy. Much of the science we need to shape policy for babies and their families is actually already a few decades old. We've seen the effects of this mismatch between knowledge and policy coming for a long time. What have we been waiting for?

One oft-cited reason for delay is lack of funding. That only looms larger in the current economic climate. Yet for years now Lally and others, including some of the economists cited in this book, have shown how investments in quality early education and preventive healthcare will more than pay for themselves when children reach adulthood. This bottom-line wisdom has begun to spread but won't go far enough as long as the business world's cycle goes from quarter to quarter and the political one only looks 4 years down the road. The return on this investment takes longer than that, but too many of our institutions are focused on the short term only. And as Lally says, the total investment cost is so trivial relative to other budget items that the issue really isn't money at all. The issue is priorities.

Lally is reluctant to use this economic argument for investing in children because he believes the moral one should suffice to make this a priority. Shouldn't we do everything we can to protect our babies, whether it saves money or not? Not everyone thinks so. The moral path leads to different priorities depending on one's fundamental belief system. For example, Lally points to the strongly held belief that families should take care of themselves on their own as an obstacle to science-informed early childhood policies. Yet such beliefs cannot be displaced by simply citing the moral position that Lally and many of us share, nor by an appeal to science, which is regarded skeptically by many who harbor these beliefs.

We have a cultural divide in our country: Science is on one side, certain ideological beliefs on the other. Individualism and the greater good are polarized, too. The urgent changes that Lally, others, and we have called for over the years may not occur until we can learn to listen and understand across the divide and reach for common ground. This book is a starting place for urgently needed dialogue that will finally lead to action.

We believe that beneath these differences, Americans will find common values and goals, and shared concerns about the weakening of families, neighborhoods and communities; the erosion of values by a consumption-driven economy; and the consequences of these for the future of our country. Although we may disagree about the details, there is a growing understanding on both sides of this divide that professionals, families, and communities need each other, and we need better policies to raise the next generation. Until recently, the gulf between those who feel a moral obligation to all children and those who limit themselves to those they are related to by genes or adoption was wide. Now, though, on both sides of the aisle there is a new call to protect *our* children's futures—whether from future federal debt or from inadequate health care and education in the present.

What is new is that we have arrived at a crossroads—a critical period for our nation's development when the choices we make now will either lead to a prosperous future or condemn us to stagnation and decline. Not only have our babies been neglected, but our families, neighborhoods, schools, and health care system have too. Too many babies born in the 1980s and 90s are now adults who cannot meet the challenges of the global competitive workforce. Too many have become parents whose brains were not prepared in early childhood to allow them to nurture their own babies' brains. If we do not act now, we will soon tip into a point of no return with too few healthy and well-educated adults in this country to protect it and keep it strong. For decades, along with Ron Lally and others, we have been calling for leaders to act on what we know. What is different now is that, in addition to the scientific evidence, our nation faces the kind of urgent crisis that may finally push our leaders to act.

We all want a prosperous future for our country and our children. Out of these dire times may come a powerful new consensus that to accomplish this we must raise all of our children to grow up to become adults who have the resilience to cope with adversity, strengthen their communities, engage as active participants in civic life, steward our fragile planet's limited resources, and nurture the next generation to be prepared to do the same.* We are grateful to Ron Lally for this book and his life's work to advance this critical mission.

—T. Berry Brazelton, MD, & Joshua Sparrow, MD
November 27, 2012
Harvard University

---

*Adapted from the Brazelton Touchpoints Foundation Mission Statement.

Preface

It has been 46 years since I started working with babies, and I never thought I would have to write a book of this nature—not in the United States. But it seems that, in spite of all of the "children are our most important resource" rhetoric, the fact is that, in the United States, the needs of young children, particularly babies, are being ignored to the point of neglect. Every day, neuroscience research is accumulating more evidence that each human's intellectual, emotional, perceptual, and communicative capabilities are dependent on brain structures formed during the first 3 years of life. Recent discoveries have shown that babies' early life experiences construct a foundation for learning capability in preschool, throughout school, and long after formal schooling has ended.

As a country, we're doing little to support babies and their parents through this critical period of learning. We consistently back away from taking the necessary, science-recommended steps to ensure that our youngest are placed on a path toward productive citizenry. In fact, the way we treat babies currently leaves much of their development to chance or places them at risk.

What is alarming is that most Americans have no idea that the United States falls well behind most other countries in the support that it provides infants. For example, did you know that the United States is the only industrialized country not to have a national paid-leave policy for parents at and around the birth of a child? Did you know that American families pay an average of 80% of child-care costs, while European families pay an average of 30% (Lally, 2010)? Did you know that in 1971 only a veto by then-President Richard Nixon prevented the United States from having family support services similar to the rest of the industrialized world?

This book will bring to light the harmful aspects of America's treatment of its babies that have been invisible to most of us. It will share research about recently discovered sensitive periods in infant development, during which particular environments and experiences are needed to prevent developmental damage. It will present the current realities American families face while negotiating pregnancy, dealing with delivery, handling care at home during the earliest months, and searching for and securing out-of-home child care. It will share the words of parents who are desperately trying to patch together services so that their children won't be damaged by their absence during critical bonding times or receive low-quality care. It will show how the informal supports (e.g., availability of extended family; one parent at home) that many families of the past relied upon when raising children have disappeared and how the United States, unlike many other countries, has not developed formal supports in their place. It will present the work of distinguished economists that shows how attending to early development can actually save the country money.

Since the 1950s, and without consciously choosing to do so, America has negatively altered the early experiences of our babies. In effect, we've allowed babies to shoulder the impact of massive social changes in gender equity, work, family structure, and child care, all with little assistance from the larger society.

The way we treat babies in the United States squanders precious opportunities and wastes precious lives. We can no longer afford to let the poor treatment babies receive remain invisible. How babies are treated while they are in the womb, after birth in developing attachment relationships with those who care for them, and while being cared for by people other than their family members—all of it affects the development of their brains, their functioning in school, and their productivity as citizens. My hope is that, once you finish this book, you will join me in demanding that America stop neglecting its babies and provide adequate support for the development of its youngest citizens.

Acknowledgments

I would like to express my appreciation to Glen Harvey and the Executive Team at WestEd for their support of my time while writing this book. I thank Evelina Du, Denise Grosberg, and Julie Weatherston for their help with all stages of book development. Their work has been excellent and untiring. I thank Catherine Tsao for the superb research she conducted, which led to the development of Chapters 3 through 6. I thank Katie Ranftle and Susan Liddicoat for their wise, thoughtful editing. I thank Marie Ellen Larcada, of Teachers College Press, for her encouragement to write a book on this topic. I thank my wife, Lauren, for the unwavering support she provided to me throughout the writing process. Finally, I would like to thank the mothers and fathers from across the country who were willing to participate in intensive interviews about their experiences of carrying, delivering, and raising a baby in the United States of America.

For Our Babies

PART I

Recognizing the Importance of Support for Babies and Their Families

CHAPTER 1

A Society Changes;
Its Thinking and Policies Don't

> Families are not now, nor were they ever, the self-sufficient
> building blocks of society, exclusively responsible,
> praiseworthy, and blamable for their own destiny. They are
> deeply influenced by broad social and economic forces over
> which they have little control.
>
> —Kenneth Keniston. "The Myth of Family Independence"

In the United States, attitudes relating to caring for young children and the supports we provide them are grounded in the past. We raise children and design family support policies based on ideas that are sometimes centuries old. For example, no matter how many studies show the reality to be different, the American view of a normal family leans toward the idealized *Leave It to Beaver* family structure of the 1950s. Similarly, many of our beliefs about children's development and how best to rear children are built on antiquated theories that, while proven inaccurate by recent science, still influence both individuals and governments. Unfortunately, when national or state policies to assist families are built on inaccurate theories of child development and outdated notions of family life, the policies don't fit the real needs of families. What we experience in the 21st century is a battle between child development facts (research-based information), fictions (unverified beliefs), and outdated assumptions about family functioning that keep the United States from adequately supporting early development. Chapter 2 addresses the unverified beliefs by introducing the latest science on infant development. This chapter will explore common child-rearing beliefs and practices that are rooted in the past, and take a look at families as they were in the 1950s and 1960s and as they are now.

COMMONLY HELD UNVERIFIED THEORIES OF CHILD REARING

Everyone who cares for a child or shapes policy for care operates—consciously or not—from theories that direct his or her approach to child rearing. These theories include beliefs about how children develop and function, what they need, what motivates them, and how they should be treated. They also drive the shaping of policies and practices deemed appropriate for the care of all children. What follows are summaries of commonly held theories that hold sway in the United States, influencing how we treat our children and plan policies for their care (adapted from Lally, 2006):

- *Natural Unfolding/Noble Savage.* Based in part on the work of the 18th-century French social and political philosopher Jean-Jacques Rousseau, this theory views children as fundamentally good souls who need to be protected from the damaging messages of society. Rather than trying to shape children's behavior to meet societal standards, one should let them blossom. A child does not need to have his or her natural urges controlled or shaped in order to develop into a contributing member of society. Instead, adults need to resist interfering with a child's natural growth process and allow for the child's unfolding. This "nature gospel" of education was quite popular in the United States in the late 1960s and early 1970s and has inspired pedagogical methods worldwide.
    This approach works very well for meeting the needs of the very young baby, up to about 9 months of age, by matching the baby's need for

protection, security, and emotional warmth with a giving and forgiving parenting style. However, it does little to provide the developmentally appropriate guidance in relating to others that children need at about 15 to 30 months. Just when a child's brain is primed for help with the crucial issues of impulse control, emotional regulation, empathy, and distinguishing the needs and rights of self from those of others, this theory leaves children to their own devices.

- **Tabula Rasa/Blank Slate/Empty Vessel.** This theory views the child as coming into the world without predisposed inclinations—as a "blank slate." Dating back to Aristotle, it gained popularity over the centuries through the writings of philosopher John Locke and behaviorist B. F. Skinner. It posits that how a child turns out is completely based on his or her experiences and environment and the information provided through interactions with others. This theory gives little credence to scientifically proven concepts such as temperamental differences and biological predisposition. Many policymakers and politicians who are committed to seeing all children obtain basic academic skills hold to this notion. They believe it's possible to just write on the blank slate with a good deal of content, paying little attention to individual temperament, biological makeup, or personal learning style.

- **The Tempted (Devil on the Left Shoulder—Angel on the Right).** This theory arises from religious principles and argues that children are constantly tempted by competing messages: do selfish, evil things or selfless, good things. Adults who espouse this theory see their role as helping children be vigilant and resist temptation in order to live a good and productive life. To keep a child from falling victim to messages of the "devil," the adult becomes a reinforcing voice of the "angel," warning children away from temptations. This often dampens child inclinations toward questioning, creativity, and experimentation.

- **Unsocialized Savage.** Derived from Puritan ideology, this theory proposes that, unless impulses are strongly inhibited and controlled from birth, a child will move into adulthood as an unsocialized and uncivilized being. Early urges, if not checked, will create an adult who is greedy, unethical, and overly sexual—someone who seeks only personal pleasure and gain. Thus, it is the duty of responsible adults to control children's willfulness and stifle acting-out urges with stern, powerful, and consistent discipline. This theory encourages starting adult control of child behavior as early as possible, to break self-will and keep the child from starting on a destructive developmental trajectory. There is evidence that parenting and teaching practices informed by this theory, particularly when started in the child's early infancy, lead to mental health problems, poor self-image, and aggression toward others (Lally, 2006).

- **The Early Unformed.** This theory is based on a belief that infants don't perceive or understand what is happening around them. Adults who buy into it feel free to do almost anything in the child's presence, or to not interact with them very much. This theory assumes that young children have little intellectual capability and that most of what happens (or doesn't happen) around them—for example, loud televisions, screaming fights within earshot, or isolation in a crib or playpen—will have no lasting effect or permanent consequence for them. Followers of this theory may wonder why they should talk to or point things out to a child whose mind barely works. This approach to early child rearing leads to insecure attachment, stifles the child's intellectual and linguistic development, and is often linked to abuse and neglect.

- **The Innocent.** According to this theory, until children reach an "age of reason" at age 6 or 7, they are innocent and unmotivated by inappropriate thoughts and feelings; therefore, they should not be held responsible for their actions. Adults who view young children as innocents believe it to be inappropriate to provide them with behavioral expectations and limits. They will often give a 2- or 3-year-old child free rein to explore, to choose how and with what to play, and to "be a child." Once the child reaches the age of reason, however, adults' expectations regarding children's behavior shift suddenly, and so do the discipline techniques and education practices used. In implementing this theory, adults often lose sight of how crucial their guiding interactions with children are for creating appropriate socialization in the second and third years of life.

A contrasting, science-based theory, "The Vulnerable Competent Learner," cna be found in Chapter 2.

THE CHANGING AMERICAN FAMILY

We as a nation must come to grips with the fact that the family configurations and work patterns common in the 1950s barely still exist. Across the last 60 years, the nation has experienced a gradual erosion of the supports families once received from their extended families, neighborhoods, and communities. These supports, though informal, were critical to the fabric of everyday family life. By looking back at life in the '50s and '60s—when family and neighborhood could serve as informal, yet solid, support systems for a new mother—we can identify the supports that have been or are being lost.

The 1950s

It's 1951, and we are on Poplar Street in Dumont, New Jersey, looking in on a young mother with a 2-year-old daughter. Eighteen months ago, shortly after she gave birth, her husband of 2 years was killed in the Korean War. Within weeks after his death, she moved out of the apartment she and her husband had rented and returned to live with her mother and father in her childhood home, among neighbors she has known most of her life. She talks with them about the ups and downs of life. Sometimes they shop together, and they often share the small things of life: tools, recipes, child-rearing advice, and homemaking tips. She also has a sister who lives close by with her two children, and a brother who lives in the same county. For the past year, she has worked part-time as a secretary while her mother—or sometimes her sister or cousin—cares for her daughter. As her daughter gets older, neighbors have begun to ask if her daughter can play at their homes with their children.

Her family usually celebrates birthdays, holidays, and anniversaries at her parents' home, or occasionally at her brother's or sister's. Sometimes major events may mean visiting the home of an aunt, an uncle, or a cousin. She has been a member of a church in Dumont since she was a child, and the minister counseled her and helped her through the painful time after her husband's death. It was, in fact, a fellow church member who helped her find her job. She doesn't make much money, and she thinks she can handle more responsibility at work. She sometimes feels hemmed in living in her parents' home, but she is weathering this troubled time with the knowledge that there are people nearby on whom she can depend.

This story describes how families and communities of 60 years ago would have typically responded to a single mother's emergency. The problem of a struggling parent was seen as the family's concern, with solutions that could be handled through established relationships within the extended family and community.

A Gradual Change Takes Place

In the 1950s and 1960s, the overwhelming majority of Americans lived in nuclear or extended families. During those decades, a middle-class family usually included a mother who took care of the home and children and a father working outside the home, with extended family members living in the home or close by. Of course, even then women in low-income families worked outside the home. By the 1970s, vast cultural and economic shifts meant that parents and other adults who are vital to very young children's development were becoming less and less available to them, all but erasing many of the family and community supports that existed in the '50s and '60s. As they adjusted to the gradual changes in work, family, and the roles of women in society, families didn't realize that babies were losing something essential in the process—the early adult nurturance, provided by trusted caregivers, that is necessary for healthy development—and that, to the detriment of babies, few formal, societal structures had been developed to take the place of the vanishing informal support structures.

Until the 1970s, the United States government's relationship to families was much the same as that of other industrialized nations: families were left to deal with child-rearing issues on their own. During the 1970s, however, many governments found it necessary to respond to vast social changes by increasing their involvement with families. Governments in most industrialized countries began providing formal supports for women and families to compensate for the loss of informal supports. For example, in 1971, Italy legislated the provision of fully paid leave for working mothers for a 5-month period before and after a baby's birth; support for a mother's entry or reentry into the workforce (including sick leave, health care, and flexible hours); and special assistance for poor families with young children. The United States came very close to making similar provisions for its families that same year. With bipartisan support, Congress passed the Comprehensive Child Care Act, which was comparable in content to nationwide laws then being passed in many countries. While President Nixon originally supported the act, he took back his support and issued a last-minute veto, with the justification that such supports would "sovietize" our youth (Zigler, Marsland, & Lord, 2009, p. 34). Since then, efforts to introduce the society-wide benefits common in other industrialized countries have been blocked by uniquely American arguments about the danger of such programs to the sanctity of family rights, individual choice, and responsibility, as well as by reliance on market-driven parent/provider negotiations for child-care services.

The end of the 1970s marked a watershed moment in the history of American families: For the first time, more mothers worked outside the home than in the home. By 1979, only 1 in 16 families fulfilled the breadwinner-father/homemaker-mother family model of the '50s (Human Resources and Community Development Division of the Congressional Budget Office,

1983). Families had changed so dramatically that the need was starting to show for formal supports to replace the informal supports that had eroded. The 1980s saw a continuing increase in the number of women working outside the home, including a large jump in the percentage of mothers of infants who worked outside the home. In 1984, Rep. George Miller (D-CA), chairman of the Select Committee on Children, Youth, and Families, and his colleagues recommended sweeping changes to our country's family support efforts to address these shifts in work patterns. They felt that the government should respond to what they saw as the historic and long-term changes in American society, the American economy, and the American workplace (U.S. Congress, 1984). Figure 1.1 reflects these changes by illustrating how, over the years since 1960, the number of working mothers with infants has continued to increase.

The 21st Century

Let's return to our Poplar Street family. It is 2013. The 2-year-old daughter from 1951 is now a 64-year-old grandmother living in Florida. Her 36-year-old daughter moved from Chicago to Los Angeles with her son and daughter (ages

Figure 1.1. Percentage of Working Mothers with Infants: 1960–2009

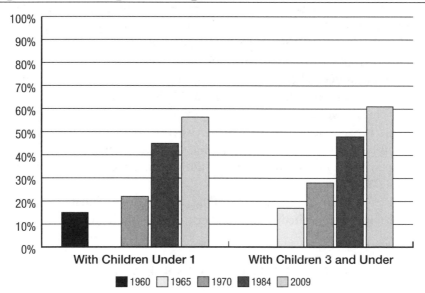

Source: Hayghe, 1984; U.S. Department of Labor, 2009

6 and 2) a year and a half ago, motivated by an opportunity for career advancement and a fresh start after a recent divorce. Her children were born after she finished college and started her career. She worked for as long as she could before they were born and returned to work right after they were born, for fear of losing her job. She likes Los Angeles and her challenging new work responsibilities, but she finds she has to give a great deal of herself at work to build professional credibility. In addition, her rent is higher than she had anticipated, and it's hard to predict her commute time to and from work. Three days a week, her daughter goes to a home-based day care while her son participates in an after-school program at the Boys Club; she has hired a sitter for the other 2 days, and her combined child-care costs are expensive. Her weekends are usually spent cleaning, shopping, doing laundry, and going on outings with the children.

Her mother visits once or twice a year, and they talk on the phone at least once a week. When her work occasionally takes her to New York City, she gets a chance to visit her cousins, who still live in New Jersey. She's only made one close friend since moving to Los Angeles, a married colleague from work; however, they seldom associate off the job because her friend's husband also works full time. She recently started dating, but fitting it in among her family life and other activities is tough.

When one of her children or one of their caregivers is sick, her whole carefully constructed system breaks down, and she has no one to turn to for support. While she looks forward to having time to herself when her children visit their father, she misses them when they are in Chicago. Her hope is that things will get easier for her as the children get older.

A sketch of middle-class family life in 2013 can vary in many ways, depending on individual circumstances. Common to most versions, however, are a mother's rush back to work after giving birth; a lack of good, reliable child care; a breakdown in family functioning whenever a child or caregiver gets sick; and the absence of informal support networks. The experience of this Los Angeles mother typifies the family-life struggles of the 56% of American mothers who are employed and have children under age 3 (U.S. Department of Labor, 2007).

Figure 1.2 provides an overview of the changes in the climate for the raising of babies in the United States between 1955 and 2013.

A LOOK AT FAMILIES WITH BABIES TODAY

Since 2007, just over 4 million babies have been born each year in the United States, and many of their mothers are working. Sixty-one percent are in the

Figure 1.2. The Changed Climate for the Young Child in American Society

	1955	2013
National Climate	Economic systems are oriented toward one-worker families. Few institutional supports for child rearing and family life. Families rely heavily on mothers, other family members, and neighbors for child-rearing assistance.	Economic systems are oriented toward individual workers. More work, consumption, and activity outside the home, but few supports for child rearing and family life. Families rely heavily on mothers; extended family and neighbors are not often available.
Neighborhood and Community Climate	Somewhat stable, with informal contact among members, and friendship networks based on proximity and family ties. Emergency help is often available. Group socialization of children. Community services are few but personal.	Changes often because of family and neighbor movement. Little contact with neighbors, and sparse feeling of neighborhood support. Emergency help is rarely available. Community services are formalized and usually impersonal.
Climate of the Young Child Within the Family	Nuclear family, with mother as principal caregiver and the child additionally cared for by relatives and close friends. Extended family members often live close by.	Increased numbers of babies live in families with the mother working outside the home but still the principal caregiver. Greatly increased occurrence of babies being formally cared for by nonrelatives and changing caregivers.

labor force, a figure that has been increasing each year, up from 57% in 2006. Significantly, in 2008, more first-time moms were working while pregnant, working later into pregnancy, and going back to work sooner than in past years. Sixty-seven percent of first-time moms worked during their pregnancy (57% of them worked full time), 80% worked during the month before they gave birth, and 55% were working 6 months after they gave birth (Centers for Disease Control and Prevention, 2012a). As a point of comparison, between 1961 and 1965, 41% of first-time moms worked while pregnant, 35% worked during the month they gave birth, and only 14% were working 6 months after giving birth (U.S. Census Bureau, 2011).

It is noteworthy that the majority of working mothers are unhappy. Sixty-six percent of working mothers say they would rather work part-time. Their reasons include wanting to be home with their very young children, concerns about the quality of child care, and feeling constantly rushed and harried because of work/family responsibilities (Pew Research Center, 2009).

And what of today's parents' financial ability to stay home with a newborn? Only 8% of new U.S. mothers, and a statistically insignificant percentage of new fathers, are eligible to receive any paid family leave (Lovell, O'Neill, & Olsen, 2007). A survey conducted by the U.S. Department of Labor in 2000 found that 88% of those who needed and were technically eligible for family leave couldn't afford to take it (Department of Labor Bureau of Statistics, 2006). This is probably because the leave available to most families is unpaid. The Family and Medical Leave Act (FMLA) that became law in 1993 allows *unpaid* leave up to 12 weeks in any 12-month period for the birth or adoption of a child; acquiring a foster child; the serious illness of a child, spouse, or parent; and the serious illness of an employee for employees who have been employed for one year and work at least 1,250 hours (25 hours a week). Companies with fewer than 50 employees are not required to provide family and medical leave. Han and Waldfogel (2003; Waldfogel, 1999) found no change in employee leave coverage and usage since the act became law.

Paid leave however has been offered by the state of California since 2002 as part of state disability insurance. Workers who are covered by state disability insurance are also eligible for paid family leave. A study has shown that its availability is a key motivator for parents' decision to take leave (Gomby & Pei, 2009). Yet only 8% of new U.S. mothers, and a statistically insignificant percentage of new fathers, are eligible to receive any paid family leave (Lovell, O'Neill, & Olsen, 2007).

With regard to where babies spend their days, 6 million U.S. children under the age of 3 are in child care, with approximately half of all children spending 25 hours a week in care (Behrman, 2001), and the care they receive is expensive. According to one recent analysis, the average annual cost of center-based infant care consumes almost 20% of a household's average take-home pay (National Association of Child Care Resource and Referral Agencies, 2006).

Finally, looking at the fate of babies currently being born in the United States, too many of them are struggling for life from the start. In a 20-year analysis of newborn death rates around the world, a study published in *Pediatrics* showed that the United States ranked 41st out of 45 industrialized countries, on par with Qatar and Croatia (Meara, Kotagal, Atherton, & Lieu, 2004).

THE NEEDS OF THE CHANGED FAMILY

Families raising infants and toddlers have always needed support, but with the number of women in the workforce increasing and the informal supports of the 1950s and 1960s rarely available, raising young children has become quite difficult. In the United States, there is an almost impossible expectation for parents to be able to both work and provide sufficient nurturance without societal support.

The problems families with babies face are much wider and deeper than any individual family can handle on its own. However, Americans' strongly held beliefs about the sanctity of the family in child-rearing matters and concerns about the loss of individual freedoms are standing in the way of providing babies with the supports they so desperately need. These beliefs, coupled with attitudes that treat out-of-home infant and toddler care as a babysitting business (with caregivers receiving minimal wages and very little training) rather than an important education enterprise, have made life for babies and their parents in the United States very difficult.

I am not going to address the multitude of reasons why more mothers of infants and toddlers are moving into or staying in the out-of-home workforce despite having few supports to assist them. Nonetheless, this trend has created serious, widespread problems for modern families, which exceed the realm of the personal solution. The situations these families tangle with daily are part of a nationwide phenomenon caused by 60 years of massive social change, and they require social solutions. Work and home life exist within a broad social context that includes laws, employment practices, economics, and technological influences. Asking individual families to solve such problems on their own is expecting too much. The big problem underlying individual day-to-day problems is this: American society hasn't done enough to support families as the roles of family members have changed. Formerly effective supports, once widely available in society, have diminished as the need for help has grown.

How are families affected by these changing realities? To close this chapter, four comments from mothers interviewed for this book (between 2008 and 2012) offer a window into what families across the country experience while raising babies in the United States:

> It felt against my instinct to leave my baby, and I did not feel like that was what I was supposed to be doing, yet I wanted to have a career at the same time. . . . I know a lot of other nurses I work with take the full 12 [weeks] and they come back to work in tears. And you ask them, "How

are you doing?" And they say, "Don't even ask. Don't even ask because I'll just break down crying." And I know other women that this is not long enough for either.

Because I've chosen to reduce my hours, it's sort of like, "You're not the person we thought you were. We thought you were this person that was going to be there for the business and bleed for the business."

My husband and I live pretty far away from various relatives who would otherwise be helping, and if I lived near my mom, for example, right now, all these times that I'm just completely wiped out and I have to lie down because I'm having contractions and I'm trying to take care of my toddler, mom could have just come over and helped out.

He (an 11-month-old boy) is currently in a day care with 12 babies in a room with two caregivers, which is completely unacceptable and downright frightening as a mother. It is sickening to know that he spends 10 hours a day with caretakers who might or might not give him the love, care, and attention he needs. I know I am probably overreacting, but how do I know he is being held enough or nurtured properly when I hear reports of him crying all day or not taking his bottles because he prefers and needs to be with me and be nursed by me? I am so afraid that I have cheated my son out of the most crucial time in his life to have proper care, and there is nothing that I can do about it now except count down the days until June [she is a teacher], when he can return to my arms. Only time will tell.

CHAPTER 2

How the New Brain Research Changes Everything!

We must remember. The first few years of life are not a rehearsal. This is the real show. Children do not really have an opportunity to try to get it right later.

—Irving Harris, *Should Public Policy Be Concerned with Early Childhood Development?*

School readiness, a competent workforce, solid taxpayers, fewer criminals, people able to get along with each other—all of these characteristics of a healthy, productive society have their origins in infancy. Why? Because, unlike other organs, the brain is not fully formed at birth. When we are born, our brains are only 25% of the size of the adult brain and still under construction, developing all of the connections we'll rely upon for success in life.

Throughout infancy our brains go through a period of rapid construction. By age 3, they have grown to 85% of adult size. The experiences people go through during the first few years of life shape how their brains will function later, and, amazingly, early experiences not only increase the brain's size but influence its physical structure. It's been found that these early experiences influence how genes release chemicals that shape our brains. Genes shape the brain in reaction to experience, to prepare it for similar experiences. These early gene/environment interactions—including how one is treated as a baby and the conditions in which one is raised—"tell" the genes how to prepare the brain for its future, building the foundations for how one will think, feel, and communicate. When these experiences are nurturing and in tune with a baby's inborn needs and expectations, the structures that are built support the development of such abilities as self-regulation, curiosity, speech, and emotional attachment to others. When these experiences are not nurturing, they can wire the brain to be, among many other negative outcomes, hyper-vigilant (stressfully searching for signs of danger) and/or withdrawn (shying away from contact with others). In the short term, these traits may be useful safety mechanisms that protect a child from real and immediate risks, but if incorporated as a long-term mode of addressing the world, they are likely to limit the child's future growth. By the time a child is 3 years old, some early patterns of thinking and feeling are already ingrained and difficult to change. In fact, these patterns of thinking and feeling, if wired into the brain at an early age, can last a lifetime. This is why we must, as a society, pay early attention to the daily experiences of babies.

THE BRAIN'S NEED FOR A "SOCIAL WOMB"

Unlike the brains of most other species, the brains of human beings con-tinue to form after birth, going through a long period of extrauterine ges-tation (Hamburg, 1995; Lawson, 2010). Just as the fetus needed the safety of the womb in which to grow, the human brain needs a "social womb," an environment that both protects it from harm and informs it about suc-cessful functioning in the specific social and cultural environment into which it is delivered (Schore, 2001a). While a duck can quickly go about its business once hatched, being born with a small, immature brain leaves human infants completely dependent on adult caregivers for at least their first 2 years. Hamburg (1995) describes this vulnerable period of early brain growth as a "prolonged helplessness" that, rather than being a weakness, is one of human infants' greatest strengths. Through this dependence, they learn more about functioning in the world *after* they come out of the womb than any other animal.

Babies depend on caregivers and the environments in which they receive care to establish a basic wiring of the brain that prepares the brain for what is to come. By seeking out their caregivers and participating in learning experiences with them, babies shape their brains to function in the *particular* physical and social environments of those who care for them (Schore, 2003, 2005; Spence, Shapiro, & Zaidel, 1996; Thompson, 2009). The human brain is engaged in generation-by-generation adaptation. Having a brain not fully formed at birth really is an asset. It allows human beings to build their brains to adjust to current conditions (life in the current generation and environmental circumstances), cultures (family and community values), and technologies (language, tools, utensils, etc.).

As the young brain grows, it builds the structures for how a child will think, feel, and learn in the future (Spence et al., 1996). As I noted earlier, an infant's brain is, at birth, smaller and much less complex than the adult brain. By the end of toddlerhood, however, it has gone through a major structural transformation. It is closer to the adult brain in both size and wiring, and it is also more prepared to leave the social womb and take on the world. This early brain-building process means that people and surroundings are extremely critical factors for a baby's later success in life.

HOW DID SCIENTISTS LEARN ABOUT THE INFANT BRAIN?

In the last 20 years there have been dramatic changes in the technology available to study babies' development. These advances mean we're no longer forced to guess about the goings-on in a young child's brain; we can now actually see what is happening (Rogers, Morgan, Newton, & Gore, 2007). As recently as the 1950s, scientists were dissecting brains from cadavers to gain a better understanding of how they functioned. In the '60s and '70s, much of what we learned about how infant brains developed was the product of ingenious experiments in psychological laboratories. Since psychologists couldn't actually see what was going on in the brain—which they referred to as the "black box" (Aubrun & Grady, 2002)—they had to infer brain activity by observing the infant's behavioral responses to carefully selected stimuli. This type of innovative psychological experimentation helped (and is still helping) researchers make many discoveries about the early competencies and vulnerabilities of babies. For example, an experiment testing whether young babies act with intention linked a pacifier to a mechanism that could bring a photo into focus. When a young baby was given a choice among several projected photos and repeatedly sucked the pacifier to make one clearer than the others, it could be assumed that the infant had the intention to do so (Kalnins & Bruner, 1973). As a result of such studies, scientists came to understand babies as much more involved with, influenced by, and interested in influencing their environments than previously imagined.

Scientists have also generated theories about human brains by making inferences based on studies of the monkey brain that used implanted electrodes to gather data on brain functions. Such implants were, of course, too intrusive to use with human brains, making it impossible to have absolute certainty about human brain function. This uncertainty often led to researchers making inaccurate inferences. For example, as recently as 1980, many neuroscientists thought that the structure of a human baby's brain couldn't change in response to experiences but was instead determined by genetics and fixed at birth.

Today, with advanced, nonintrusive imaging technology (see Figure 2.1), scientists can see inside the "black box." These new technical tools have helped scientists pinpoint areas of the brain responsible for specific functions and observe the human brain as it operates.

When used with human subjects, these noninvasive techniques allow scientists to see neurons firing in the brain at the exact moment a sensory event, motor action, or cognitive activity takes place. Scientists can now identify which areas of the brain are activated during various experiences, and at what level of intensity. In this way, they've been able to build a very detailed and accurate picture of how the human brain functions and how it can be altered during early development. For example, watching blood pulse through the arteries of the fetal brain's left and right hemispheres, scientists can discern that the flow substantially increases in the left hemisphere when a mother hums or recites a nursery rhyme. This suggests that this hemisphere is preprogrammed to respond to auditory signals (Hykin et al., 1999), something that was never known until this technology was created. Using fMRI technology, scientists can better pinpoint the roles of different areas of the brain, seeing specific parts "light up" from use when a baby responds to various stimuli.

Each of these new technological tools has given researchers a much better understanding of the purposes of various parts of the human brain, as well as how the environment activates neurons—and there's more. Amazingly,

Figure 2.1. New Nonintrusive Ways of Studying the Human Brain

Positron Emission Tomography (PET)	• Measures glucose levels in the brain • Applications include the assessment of brain function and evaluation of brain abnormalities
Functional Magnetic Resonance Imaging (fMRI)	• Measures blood flow in the brain • Applications include the production of activation maps showing which parts of the brain are involved in a particular mental process while they are working
Near-Infrared Spectroscopy (NIRS)	• Measures light in the brain • Applications include the assessment of blood flow in the front part of the brain and brain activity
Transcranial Magnetic Stimulation (TMS) and Magnetoencephalography (MEG)	• Measures electrical impulses in the brain • Applications include basic research on perceptual and cognitive brain processes, localizing regions affected by pathology, determining the function of different brain regions, and neurofeedback

technology makes it possible to watch the brain form. Scientists can now see brain cells as they migrate from the base of the brain to the part of the brain where the cell will serve its highly specific function for the rest of a person's life; they can also see what disrupts that migration (Lenroot & Giedd, 2006). It is possible to track how connections between brain cells are pruned due to disuse or, when used, are stimulated to form complex and robust pathways for efficient functioning (Bruer, 1997).

There has also been an explosion of information about the importance of complex gene-experience interactions to brain structure and function. Because scientists are now capable of observing activity inside a gene and have the ability to isolate, splice, and modify genes, they've recently learned that (1) early experience can influence the way genes are expressed and (2) gene expression influences both brain structure and processing capacity (Greenspan, 1990; Meaney, 2001; Sroufe, 1996). For example, researchers have found that early emotional and social deprivation can impact gene expression in ways that set neural pathways to significantly and negatively alter brain functioning (Meaney, 2001), including future thinking and feeling capacity (Sroufe, 1996). Because of this new technology, we now have conclusive scientific evidence that babies' brains are significantly shaped by their early experiences and environments, proving that the quality of the interactions they have with those who provide their early care can change the structure of their brains (Schore, 2005).

MAKING CRUCIAL INFORMATION ABOUT
INFANCY AVAILABLE TO THE GENERAL PUBLIC

In the 1990s, understanding of the impact of experience on early development began to extend beyond research laboratories and find a much larger audience. Three brain-related conferences held between 1994 and 1997 helped disseminate new scientific knowledge about early brain development and link it to recommendations for new child-care policies and practices. The first of these conferences trumpeted the release of a groundbreaking piece, *Starting Points: Meeting the Needs of Our Youngest Children* (Carnegie Corporation of New York, 1994), and, for the first time, brought research on babies' brains to the attention of a nonscientific audience. The conference attendees—governors, policymakers, educators, and pediatricians—heard solid new data supporting arguments for improved child and family services.

Interestingly, although only a few pages of the report were devoted to recent brain research and the new technology making it possible, it was this topic that garnered the most attention from the national media. After the event, Chicago philanthropist Irving Harris and Michael Levine, the Carnegie staff member behind *Starting Points*, decided that the information on early brain development needed to be made available to a much wider audience. They decided to conduct another conference, exclusively focused on sharing and distributing the latest information on the influence of experience on early brain growth. To do so, they brought together professionals from the neuroscience, medicine, education, human services, media, business, and public policy fields for a conference held at the University of Chicago in June 1996. This conference, entitled "Brain Development in Young Children: New Frontiers for Research, Policy, and Practice," gained even more media attention than the first, in part due to the wide distribution of *Rethinking the Brain: New Insights into Early Development* (Families and Work Institute, 1996). This document, developed by the Families and Work Institute, summarized key information from the conference.

What followed was a frenzy of brain-related public information and advocacy activity that sparked an important third conference. On April 17, 1997, then-President Clinton hosted "The White House Conference on Early Childhood Development and Learning: What New Research on the Brain Tells Us About Our Youngest Children." This conference, delivered via satellite to libraries, schools, and other organizations across the United States, highlighted new scientific findings on brain development and pointed to the importance of children's earliest experiences in providing them with a strong and healthy developmental foundation.

The dissemination of new knowledge on brain research really reached its peak with the 2000 publication of *From Neurons to Neighborhoods: The Science of Early Childhood Development* (Shonkoff & Phillips, 2000). For a 2-and-a-half-year period before its publication, the National Academy of Sciences charged a committee of 17 professionals with evaluating and integrating the current science of early childhood development, and sought out leading researchers and practitioners in related professions to provide scientific input to the committee. Dozens of scientists submitted articles, papers, chapters, and books for analysis. What took form in *From Neurons to Neighborhoods* were scientifically-based answers (presented in clear language understandable to parents, practitioners, and policymakers) to two questions:

- How do infants learn and develop?
- How is learning and development best supported?

The core concepts, conclusions, and recommendations of *From Neurons to Neighborhoods* still stand as a blueprint for greatly needed actions. (This report is available online at http://www.nap.edu/books/0309069882/html/.)

Since the publication of *From Neurons to Neighborhoods*, the need to support children's early growth has only become more obvious. New research has uncovered capacities in babies at younger and younger ages and shown greater evidence of the need for adult nurturance and support throughout every stage of infancy. For example, using brain imaging, researchers at Emory University have found that the brain prepares for early intellectual interaction even before birth, becoming primed to pay attention to and respond to the spoken word (evidenced by witnessing lowered heart rate). Within minutes of birth, babies more closely attend to familiar voices than to unfamiliar voices. These researchers also found children as young as 2 months displaying discriminatory abilities, preferring to watch faces (and facelike images) rather than non-facelike images and, more specifically, watching their mother's face longer than a female stranger's face (Loftus, 2006; Rochat, 2004).

The public has long known that babies are desperately dependent upon adults for nurturance, support, security, and the provision of appropriate environments, but now it is learning the depth of babies' vulnerability. For example, even before a woman conceives, her nutrition, stress, and overall health can impact a fetus's potential development (Dacey & Travers, 2002; Lambers & Clarke, 1996; Santrock, 1995, 2006). Because the brain is not fully formed at birth, its vulnerability to environmental enrichment or assault after birth is similar to that of internal organs, such as the heart and the lungs, while still in the womb (Santrock, 1995).

DISCOVERING CRITICAL AND SENSITIVE PERIODS IN BRAIN DEVELOPMENT

In the last few years, we've learned definitively that, from conception, babies are "programmed" to expect and depend on certain kinds of experiences happening at particular times in their development. These are referred to as *critical periods*—time periods from which permanent damage can result unless certain experiences happen. Particularly in the area of perceptual development, Meaney (2001) found critical periods when the presence or absence of an experience can result in irreversible brain structuring of a young infant's hearing and speech. Siegler, DeLoache, and Eisenberg found them in vision. For example, the critical period of human's development of binocular vision (both eyes used together) is between 3 and 8 months. If the child doesn't have visual experience during that time period the eyes will always have trouble working together (Siegler, DeLoache, Eisenberg, 2006).

In other developmental domains, such as language, social, and emotional development, *sensitive periods* exist when the brain is particularly responsive to and in need of certain patterns of activity (Spence et al., 1996). Although special attention can repair these sensitive structures, compensatory experience later in life, even if only a few months later, often isn't as beneficial as having the appropriate experience happen during the initial sensitive period (Knudsen, 2004).

Many of these sensitive experiences involve how babies are treated and related to by others, and what researchers are uncovering on this front can be startling. For example, in his study of children from Romanian orphanages, Charles Nelson (2007) found that orphans placed in foster homes before their second birthday often recovered from serious developmental problems, diminished IQ, and trouble with forming emotional attachments, while those who were placed in foster homes at a later point rarely did. In another study of these same Romanian orphanages, Stacy Drury, a researcher from Tulane University, and her colleagues found that lack of experience or inappropriate experience can even alter gene structure. She discovered that, among the children from Nelson's study, the telomeres (the protective caps that sit on the end of chromosomes) of those who spent more time at the orphanages were damaged and shorter compared to those of children who left the orphanages earlier. Drury and colleagues speculated that one reason for this was that the children placed in foster homes earlier recovered because of the reduced damaging impact of early experience on their genes. Her hypothesis is that these damaged telomeres changed the architecture of the brain while it was being formed (Drury et al., 2010). Allan Schore, a researcher at UCLA, has reinforced these findings through his work, which showed that while the brain is still being formed, particularly during the first 2 years of life, the absence of nurturing and supportive environments leads to the development of faulty early brain structures, which require ingenious and complex interventions to improve (Schore, 2001a, 2001b, 2003, 2005).

New social/emotional research is also uncovering early experience triggers for heretofore-unknown vulnerabilities and competencies, such as infant depression and early expressions of empathy (Spence et al., 1996; Thompson, 2009). It is becoming obvious that the absence of certain experiences and environments, or their replacement with experiences that are incongruent with the child's needs during the period from conception to age 3, thwarts brain development (Knudsen, 2004). These findings are summarized in Figure 2.2.

Figure 2.2. A Research-Based Vision of Early Development and How It Is Best Supported

- Babies are hardwired with competencies previously unknown to science, and filled with expectations for certain types of interactions at particular points in time.
- They possess a genetically-wired learning agenda that drives them to seek and make meaning from their environment, initiate communication, make social contact, and learn language.
- They are biologically programmed to emotionally attach to, imitate, and learn from their caregivers.
- They are completely dependent upon adults for nurturance, support, and security.
- They need adults not only to help them survive, as we have always known, but to provide them with experiences that build their brains.

Source: Lally, 2011

These and other recent discoveries have led to a new theory of child rearing. I call it the *Vulnerable Competent Learner*. This theory sees children as entering the world with brains genetically wired to learn and programmed to attach to and socialize with those who care for them. It sees children as inclined to learn language and trying to make sense of the world, with motivation and curiosity genetically built into them. At the same time, adults who follow this theory recognize that babies are desperately dependent. Those who care for children using this approach understand that it is their responsibility to provide nurturance, support, and security; create a developmentally appropriate context for learning; and guide children's social development. They see themselves in a role that facilitates children's learning by protecting and nurturing them in their vulnerability and acknowledging and engaging their competencies.

GIVEN WHAT WE KNOW, WE MUST RESPOND

Early experience is the soil in which the young brain grows; it directly influences the physical construction of the brain (Spence et al., 1996). We know that it plays a powerful role in how genes are expressed and how that expression wires the brain. It's increasingly clear that, beginning in the womb, environmental factors influence the quality of how a person will think and feel later in life (Schore, 2005). We've discovered that babies come into the world programmed with the expectation that their own inborn learning and developmental agenda will be engaged and respected, and that babies are active participants in this learning agenda—imitating, interpreting, integrating, exploring, inventing, initiating communication, seeking meaning, and building relationships (Shonkoff & Phillips, 2000). We have found out that babies desperately need both nurturance and timely and appropriate experience for their brains to develop strong initial structures. Genomics, molecular biology, and neuroscience show that, as the brain grows bigger and wires itself, it uses early experiences to build future expectations, and we understand that high-quality (i.e., emotionally and intellectually appropriate) experience positively shapes the brain's architecture (Lally, 2009; Schore, 2003; Spence et al., 1996).

With all of this knowledge, it's now evident that much of what gets in the way of successful functioning in later years can be linked to missed lessons, undeveloped skills, and detrimental experiences that shaped the early development of the brain. It is now no longer debatable that what happens in the womb and in infancy has a long-lasting impact and that, as children get older, their brains operate on the foundations structured in infancy. Even in later life, when an adult brain is called on to process sophisticated experiences in a high-functioning manner, it will depend on and use the early foundational structures developed in childhood to effectively process new information (Dawson, Ashman, & Carver, 2000).

If strong structures are built in the earliest stages of development, the brain is adequately prepared to build more complex structures for future functioning. Conversely, if strong structures are not built in infancy, the odds are that future development, later in life, will take place on shaky ground.

With the preponderance of information now available, it's clear that we must not continue treating babies as we have for the last few generations. By building the right foundations during critical and sensitive early developmental periods, we'll increase the chances of successful functioning later in life. Without consistent and timely adult support, babies will flounder (Schore, 2005).

Given the human development process, it is imperative to understand that "right from the start" really does mean as early as possible and that we must start "education" very early in life. With the foundations of competence in numeracy, literacy, communication, critical thinking, social interaction, and emotional regulation built through early experience (Lally, 2009; Schore, 2003; Spence et al., 1996), cultivating a child's capacity for learning in elementary school, or even in preschool, is not enough. This cultivation requires attention even before the child is born. Yet few in the United States—including parents and educators—pay as much attention to developing learning capacity in infants as they do to developing capacity in third or fourth graders. Instead, it's common practice to depend largely on luck to deliver children to the schoolhouse door with brains primed for learning. If we are serious about promoting better academic outcomes for our children and making them more productive citizens, it is imperative that we wake up and look at what kind of beings infants really are and what they need, as I discuss in more detail in Chapters 3 through 6.

We must change our course of treatment of babies and act on this new information. This will require parents, child development professionals, and policymakers to let go of some of their long-held beliefs about young children that recent research has shown are inaccurate, putting the science of infant development at the base of decision-making about necessary foundations for the growth of American children.

PART II

....

Understanding
Babies' Needs

CHAPTER 3

Supporting Growth During Preconception and Pregnancy

A vital and productive society with a prosperous and sustainable future is built on a foundation of healthy child development. Health in the earliest years—beginning with the future mother's well-being before she becomes pregnant—lays the groundwork for a lifetime of vitality.

—National Scientific Council on the Developing Child

So much happens early on, for good or bad, that it's never too early to start supporting the development of healthy children. For example, by just two-thirds of the way through pregnancy, all organs have been formed and a good portion of the brain's basic wiring has already been completed. By birth, the heart, kidneys, and lungs are fully developed, smaller versions of the adult organs, and brain cells have migrated to the area of the brain where they will reside for the rest of a person's life. As Thompson (2010) explains:

> While in the womb, a child's brain grows more significantly in size and function than any subsequent stage of development. Neurons are produced at an astonishing rate, migrate to their destinations within the brain, and begin to form neural connections. Damage to brain growth can occur if the child is exposed to viral infections, drugs, alcohol, or environmental hazards. A mother's malnutrition or chronic stress can also result in negative effects. (p. 2)

Even starting support at conception can be too late. The healthy development of the embryo and the first few weeks of fetal development are shaped by a woman's health and habits even before she gets pregnant. Therefore, it is important to understand that the food, drink, toxins, and experiences of a prospective mother play a crucial role in the delivery of a healthy baby and the creation of a healthy brain. Yet, up to now, public policy and education efforts haven't adequately addressed the prenatal development of the brain. If we are to protect young brains, it's vital to make the significance of protecting and nurturing the brain during the period from 3 months before conception until delivery much more apparent, and to provide routine prenatal care to all. The strategic importance of this time of life to the development of the body and the brain is no longer unknown (Thompson & Nelson, 2001). Early environmental assault can change a body, a brain, and a life forever.

THE DEVELOPMENT OF THE BRAIN WHILE IN THE WOMB

Important things are happening during the first few weeks after conception inside a pregnant woman. Before a woman even knows she's pregnant, brain cells and important neural connections begin developing. The neural tube, a precursor of the central nervous system, grows during this time. Quickly following neural tube development comes the generation, proliferation, migration, and differentiation of neurons, followed by myelination (the forming of a sheath around a nerve to allow nerve impulses to move more quickly). The timing of the prenatal components of brain development is illustrated in Figure 3.1.

Environmental factors can negatively or positively affect each of these significant developments. A mother's prolonged stresses, exposure to toxins, inadequate nutrition, and bad health all threaten prenatal brain growth. Early environmental quality also influences synaptogenesis, the formation

Figure 3.1. The Early Development of the Brain

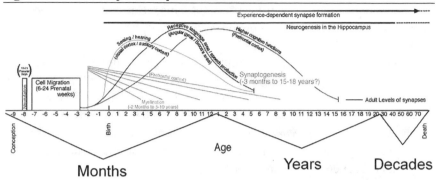

Source: Thompson & Nelson, 2001

of synapses. Although this process occurs throughout our lives, there is an explosion of synapse formation taking place during the prenatal period and early infancy. Since research has shown that some of the most devastating environmental effects on child development—including the development of the brain—happen during the prenatal period, that's when preventive efforts may have the greatest benefits (Atrash, Johnson, Adams, Cordero, & Howse, 2006; Kent, Johnson, Curtis, Hood, & Atrash, 2006; Shonkoff & Phillips, 2000; Thompson & Nelson, 2001).

NEEDED ATTENTION TO PRECONCEPTION HEALTH

Preconception health:
Most providers don't provide it.
Most insurers don't pay for it.
Most consumers don't ask for it.

—Hani Atrash, MD, MPH, *Preconception Care: Missed Opportunities to Improve Pregnancy Outcomes*

We know that protection and early intervention efforts can reduce the risks to babies' health that arise from harmful prenatal environments and stressors, but it's just as necessary to put forth similar efforts before a woman becomes pregnant. A substantial proportion of women become pregnant while experiencing poor health or engaging in bad health habits that contribute to adverse pregnancy outcomes. By the time a woman is aware she is pregnant and attends her first prenatal doctor's visit, crucial weeks have passed, and most fetal organs have already been formed. This means that the interventions needed to prevent birth defects or adverse maternal and infant outcomes often come too late to help.

There are approximately 62 million women of childbearing age in the United States. Many of these women suffer from health conditions that could contribute to adverse pregnancy outcomes. Environmental protection, early intervention, and education for women's health before pregnancy—collectively referred to as *preconception care*—can optimize pregnancy outcomes and lower pregnancy risks; starting with early prenatal care is starting too late (Atrash et al., 2006; Kent et al., 2006).

Preconception care is characterized by the need to conduct an intervention before conception, so that women can plan and prepare for pregnancies. For maximum impact, preconception care should begin at least 3 months before pregnancy. Unlike many other countries, the United States has no nationally orchestrated health-education program targeted directly toward women of childbearing age for the purpose of ensuring fetal health. Still, women of childbearing age are valid candidates for preconception care, and their babies' development would benefit from it.

Preconception Care in Other Developed Countries

At the very beginning point of potential development, before the baby is even conceived, we see the first sign of America's invisible neglect of babies. Most European countries have instituted, or are in the process of instituting, three types of supports for prenatal development:

1. A "safety net" of preconception services: obstetricians, gynecologists, or family medicine physicians who provide preconception care to the majority of women for whom they also provide prenatal care
2. Screening and treatment of depression and other mental health problems
3. An orchestrated education campaign addressing the risks of unintended pregnancies (Reeve, 2009)

For example, in 1996, the government of Hungary incorporated preconception services within its primary health-care program and increased the number of centers providing care. Its preconception services include:

- Family planning as part of a comprehensive reproductive health check-up
- A prepregnancy check-up, conducted 3 months prior to a planned pregnancy and including counseling on taking multivitamins, obtaining dental care, and behavior modification services for avoidance of alcohol and tobacco
- An early-pregnancy check-up that includes additional counseling on taking multivitamins and avoiding teratogens (agents that can produce structural or functional abnormalities in a developing embryo or fetus). Down syndrome screening is also offered (Boulet, Parker, & Atrash, 2006).

Hong Kong and South Korea also have long-standing preconception health services. Since 1998, private clinics in Hong Kong have been providing preconception care to some 4,000 couples per year; these services include pre-pregnancy counseling, health assessments and testing, and health education. The Korean Motherisk program—a hospital-based clinic established in 2004 in Seoul, South Korea—provides counseling and care for women with known risk factors who are planning a pregnancy. In addition to clinical services, the program provides preconception health promotion using TV and print media (Ebrahim, Lo, Zhuo, Han, Delvoye, & Zhu, 2006).

European countries have developed, and are continuing to develop, systems of care with the goal of comprehensive health coverage and a medical home for each parent from preconception through the perinatal period. At routine medical visits, conscious efforts are made to provide women of childbearing age with information about prepregnancy behavior that impacts a developing fetus and to provide care for risk behaviors discovered. At the first European Congress on Preconception Care and Preconception Health in Brussels on October 6–9, 2010, leaders from across Europe took as their objectives:

1. The introduction of preconception care into primary care systems in Europe
2. The sharing of information with other practitioners about effective interventions that can occur during preconception
3. Increasing awareness, among the public and policymakers, of the importance of preconception health to the developing fetus
4. The proposal of recommendations to European governments for the promotion of preconception health and care (Van der Zee et al., 2011)

European countries are currently conducting several pilot projects to improve preconception care. In one such recent program, ONE (Office of Birth and Childhood), a governmental organization serving the 5 million French-speaking people in Belgium, established a preconception care clinic and provided preconception health promotional information (posters and pamphlets) at primary care centers. An evaluation of the pilot project found that the clinics had a positive effect on raising both public and health-professional awareness of the importance of preconception health (Delvoye, Guillaume, Collard, Nardella, & Mauroy, 2008). In Italy, the International Centre on Birth Defects (ICBD) is overseeing two preconception health initiatives on behalf of the Ministry of Health: short courses on preconception care for health professionals at the national level and a population-based preconception health project, including a questionnaire to assess knowledge of preconception care; leaflets on the importance of preconception counseling, various avoidable risk factors, and folic acid requirements; and the construction of a special website with preconception health resources (Botto et al., 2005).

Lack of Preconception Care in the United States

At this time, no such efforts are underway in the United States. Alarmingly, most U.S. obstetricians, gynecologists, and general physicians ignore the opportunity to discuss the possibility of pregnancy with women of childbearing age unless the woman brings up the topic. This approach has led to the compartmentalization of information—specialists only focus on their specialties, and, if the possibility of pregnancy isn't discussed, doctors often fail to address issues related to, for example, prescription drugs that have been proven dangerous to fetal development. Also, when conducting check-ups with nonpregnant women of childbearing age, general physicians often don't include information about preparing one's body for healthy fetal development and about the damage that can be done to a fetus before a woman becomes pregnant. A March of Dimes–sponsored survey of women of reproductive age revealed that elements of preconception care, such as counseling about folic acid supplementation, are often not addressed during preventative medical visits, with only one in four women reporting having received information about folic acid from a health-care provider. Even after a public awareness campaign in the mid-90s, a survey showed that only 52% of women had ever heard of folic acid, only 9% of those women knew that folic acid helped prevent birth defects, and only 1% of all women listed folic acid intake as a way to reduce the risk of birth defects (March of Dimes Birth Defects Foundation, 2004).

Greater attention to health counseling during the preconception period can make a significant impact on women's behavior. For instance, among women not currently taking vitamin supplements on a daily basis, 89% said they would be likely to take a multivitamin if advised to do so by their health-care provider (March of Dimes Birth Defects Foundation, 2004). In reviewing patient records, Bernstein, Sanghvi, and Merkatz (2000) found that gynecological providers regularly failed to document medical histories, prescription drug use, and dietary supplements during routine gynecological visits, causing them to miss opportunities for preconception health promotion. These findings reveal that women are routinely exiting medical visits with incomplete information about the possible harmful effects of medicines or health practices on a fetus if they were to become pregnant. Similarly, although prevalence of moderate to severe depression is high (19%–48%) in women screened, current U.S. Preventive Services Task Force screening guidelines do not recommend universal screening for depression among adults, and the limited data available suggest low screening rates (U.S. Preventive Services Task Force, 2009).

Studies of preconception care in the United States have indicated that, even when preconception risks are identified, providers do not routinely provide interventions. This is despite the fact that there is extensive documentation regarding the effectiveness of several preconception interventions to address risk factors for adverse pregnancy outcomes. Interventions found to be particularly effective include folic acid supplementation; appropriate management of hyperglycemia; rubella, influenza, and hepatitis vaccination; a low-phenylalanine diet; and provision of antiretroviral medications to reduce the risk for mother-to-child HIV transmission (Reeve, 2009).

One alarming fact undermining the ability to mitigate risk factors for fetal development in the United States is that half of all U.S. pregnancies are unplanned (Centers for Disease Control and Prevention, 2012b; Jayson, 2011; National Campaign to Prevent Teen and Unplanned Pregnancy, 2012). Given this fact, many women may not realize they are pregnant in time to obtain early prenatal care, initiate preventive measures such as folic acid supplementation, or take steps to address preexisting health problems (Henshaw, 1998).

Analysis of data collected through the U.S. Pregnancy Risk Assessment Monitoring System indicates that women who had recently delivered a baby but who had not intended to become pregnant reported the following behaviors before they became pregnant: 30.9% smoked, 50.2% drank alcohol, 79.4% did not take a multivitamin, 40.1% were overweight or obese, 2% were diabetic, 8% had asthma, and 15.6% were anemic. Additionally, using 2002 and 2004 study data to assess risk factors for adverse birth outcomes among 10,066 women in both preconception and pregnancy stages, researchers found that more than half (55%) of preconception women smoked, drank alcohol frequently, and had not been tested for HIV. Nearly half (45%) of preconception women had not consumed folate-rich vegetables or folic acid, while the same was true for 20% of pregnant women (Anderson, Ebrahim, Floyd, & Atrash, 2006).

The failure to provide consistent preconception information and counseling is a glaring oversight in U.S. attempts to protect the developing fetus. If babies' development is to be protected, information and intervention services must be made more available to women before they become pregnant.

As reported by Weiss (2012), the following responses to the question "When did you see your midwife or doctor?" are, sadly, not uncommon for women in the United States:

> I was 9 weeks pregnant when I realized I was pregnant. I usually skip periods, that is why I didn't worry when I skipped two. Went to the doctor, she did a urine test and gave me a vitamin tablet.
>
> —Saartjie

> I was 10 weeks pregnant when I first saw an OB, she just gave me vitamins and told me to come back on the 2nd day next month, with my blood test and urine test results.
>
> —Ana

NEEDED ATTENTION TO
PRENATAL DEVELOPMENT DURING PREGNANCY

As stated earlier, environmental impact is extremely devastating to a fetus's health during the first weeks after conception; therefore, pregnant women's direct contact with health professionals is crucial. The course of care recommended for women prior to conception should be continued and supplemented immediately after conception and throughout the entire prenatal period, but additional direct services are also required. At conception and for approximately 2 weeks afterward, the fetus is acutely sensitive to maternal health conditions and environmental exposures, so much so that damage inflicted by outside agents and experiences during this time will be evident at birth. The fetus's sensitivity to toxic exposure remains acute through the first 60 days after conception, as organs are being formed.

Recognizing Risk Factors

Because of the potential impact of early threats from toxins and other environmental stressors, maternal health assessments should start early and include a review of all the medications, supplements, and herbal remedies currently in use by the mother-to-be (Cefalo & Moos, 1995). However, nearly 18% of women who give birth in the United States receive no prenatal care within the first 14 weeks of pregnancy, and this percentage is significantly higher among minority populations—28% among African American women, 26% among Latinas, and 32% in Native American communities (Ventura, Martin, Curtin, & Mathews, 1997).

Since the last two decades of the 20th century, adverse pregnancy outcomes have become a major public health concern in the United States. While the '70s and '80s saw steady improvements in outcomes, progress on a number of indicators has deteriorated ever since. For example, in 2002, congenital anomalies, low birth weight, preterm delivery, and maternal complications of pregnancy accounted for 46.4% of all U.S. infant deaths. Maternal complications of pregnancy didn't even appear on a 1960 list of the ten leading causes of infant mortality, but by 2002, they were the third most common cause of infant mortality in the United States, after congenital anomalies and low birth weight/ preterm delivery (Atrash et al., 2006). The United States currently ranks 41st among 45 industrialized nations in infant mortality, and the infant mortality rate is closely linked to inadequate nutrition among pregnant women. All of these figures cry out for intervention.

Figure 3.2 lists some of the fetal health risks that need to be better addressed through education and treatment during pregnancy. A more complete explanation of the dangers to the fetus from each of these conditions can be found in Appendix A.

Potential Negative Impacts of Medications and Supplements

During pregnancy, about 59% of women are prescribed a medication, other than a vitamin or mineral supplement, that might threaten the pregnancy, and use of over-the-counter medications may be even higher (Cragan et al., 2006). For example, certain anti-epilepsy drugs are known to alter normal development of the fetus, and their use during pregnancy has been associated with major malformations, growth restriction, and low IQ. Yet such

Figure 3.2. Some Risk Factors Needing to Be Addressed During Pregnancy

- Diabetes
- Hypothyroidism
- Isotretinoins (e.g., Accutane) used to treat acne
- Phenylketonuria
- Oral anticoagulants
- HIV/AIDS
- Sexually transmitted infections
- Hepatitis B
- Rubella
- Alcohol
- Absence of daily use of vitamin supplements containing folic acid
- Inadequate nutrition
- Obesity
- Smoking
- Prolonged stress
- Isolated pregnancy
- Anxiety and depression
- Causes of low-birth-weight deliveries
- Tetracycline
- Noise

risk-linked prescription medications and nonprescription supplements continue to be prescribed to and taken by pregnant women, in part due to a lack of solid information shared with pregnant women about their effect on the fetus.

One reason that women don't receive solid information on the impact of medications on pregnancy is because, in many cases, such information doesn't exist. A review conducted in 2001 concluded that there was insufficient information on fetal impact for more than 90% of prescription medications approved by the U.S. Food and Drug Administration in the previous 20 years (Lagoy, Joshi, Cragan, & Rasmussen, 2005). The gaps are even more substantial for over-the-counter and dietary supplements, which is of particular concern given that between 18% and 52% of the U.S. population takes dietary supplements (e.g., vitamin, mineral, herbal/botanical, amino acid, enzyme, protein, probiotic, glandular, or hormone-like substances), and many women use dietary supplements before and during pregnancy (Lagoy et al., 2005).

Risk Factors and Mental Health

Beyond potential impacts of medication and supplements, research is constantly revealing more and more risk factors for negative impacts on fetal development. In 2012, the American Psychological Association's *Monitor of Psychology* reported the discovery of links between prenatal risk factors and mental health problems. These links include the following:

- The incidence of schizophrenia was three times greater in people whose mothers had the flu during pregnancy.
- Maternal iron deficiency during pregnancy was found to increase the risk for schizophrenia fourfold.

- People whose mothers were undernourished when pregnant were found to have a significantly higher incidence of major affective disorders, such as mania and depression, severe enough to require hospitalization.
- Other maternal health events during pregnancy, including infections, toxin exposure, and stress, were found to boost the fetus's future risk of problems such as depression, anxiety, autism, mood disorders, and attention deficit hyperactivity disorder.
- The disruption of the inflammatory immune system caused by stressful maternal events during pregnancy can have profound effects on brain development by altering the flow of chemicals sent to the developing brain. (Weir, 2012)

Knowing as much as we know about what the external risk factors for healthy brain development are and just how impactful they can be during the critical early stages of development in the womb, it seems a waste of good brainpower to leave the fetus at the mercy of these risks.

NECESSARY SUPPORTS DURING PRECONCEPTION

If the United States wants to adequately protect the development of the fetus, we need to initiate a public information campaign for all women of child-bearing age, similar to those conducted in many European countries (Delissaint & McKyer, 2011). Such a campaign in the United States should make use of the multiple available dissemination channels, including public service announcements, social media, hospitals, health centers, doctors' offices, colleges, and the human resources departments of various agencies and businesses (Finer & Henshaw, 2006; Gestation Diabetes in France Study Group, 1991; U.S. Food and Drug Administration, 1996). In France, for example, women of childbearing age are publicly encouraged to take folic acid whether they are planning to become pregnant or not. This approach would make sense for the United States as well, because, as stated earlier in this chapter, about half of U.S. pregnancies are unplanned.

As Dr. Mary Nettleman, chairperson of the Department of Medicine in Michigan State University's College of Human Medicine, says,

> The top reason women do not seek prenatal care is they do not realize they are pregnant. In addition, women who do not realize they are pregnant will not change harmful behaviors such as drinking and smoking, which can lead to

developmental problems in newborns . . . Telling a woman she is pregnant will often cause her to immediately stop or cut down on smoking, drinking, and other behaviors that can hurt the baby. The problem is that many women do not recognize they are pregnant for several weeks, which is all it takes for the heart and brain to form. Earlier pregnancy recognition could have a huge impact on the health of newborns in this country. (Cody, 2009)

Information alone is not enough. In order to be effective in promoting fetal safety, information needs to be linked to health services for women of childbearing age, such as regular assessment, inoculation, screening, and counseling by general-practice physicians, gynecologists, and obstetricians or their staff. The U.S. Centers for Disease Control and Prevention recommend that women receive yearly assessments that include collecting information and counseling on the following topics: family health history, prior pregnancies, family concerns (e.g., domestic violence), chronic stress, diabetes, hypothyroidism, isotretinoins, phenylketonuria, oral anticoagulants, alcohol, daily use of vitamin supplements containing folic acid, adequate nutrition, obesity, and smoking. They also recommend ensuring that women have up-to-date vaccinations for hepatitis B and rubella and are screened yearly for HIV/AIDS and sexually transmitted infections (Kent et al., 2006).

NECESSARY SUPPORTS DURING PREGNANCY

As shown in Figure 3.3, 32 of the 33 nations defined as developed nations have universal health care, with the United States being the lone exception (True Cost, 2009). (Note that "universal health care" does not imply that health care is provided only by the government, as many countries implementing a universal health-care plan have both public and private insurance and medical providers.) With so much of a child's future development hinging on healthy gestation, it is imperative that the United States meet the same standard as other developed nations and ensure the availability of free or affordable health-care services to all pregnant women. Under our current laws, access to prenatal care is linked to ability to pay for it; only a lucky few are able to access the regular check-ups, assessments, counseling, and early interventions recommended by the Centers for Disease Control and Prevention. This fact has long meant that low-income, inner-city, rural, and teen mothers receive less prenatal care than other mothers (Andersen, 1968, 1995). Research has shown, however, that it is not just the number of visits

Figure 3.3. Developed Nations Providing Universal Health Care

Australia	Finland	Italy	Singapore
Austria	France	Japan	Slovenia
Bahrain	Germany	Kuwait	South Korea
Belgium	Greece	Luxembourg	Spain
Brunei	Hong Kong	Netherlands	Sweden
Canada	Iceland	New Zealand	Switzerland
Cyprus	Ireland	Norway	United Arab Emirates
Denmark	Israel	Portugal	United Kingdom

Source: True Cost, 2009

(the usual number of prenatal health visits recommended during pregnancy is between 8 and 14) but the timing and quality of the visits that makes the most difference (Walker, McCully, & Vest, 2001). If risk assessments aren't conducted at one or two of the early visits, it will be difficult to factor in individual risk levels when determining whether to extend or reduce the number of prenatal contacts before delivery.

In 2014, the United States is expected to implement a national health-care law that will greatly improve the nationwide accessibility of health care. It is recommended that, if implemented, the new health-care law include adequate coverage for preconception and prenatal services. Currently the act does not include this coverage. In addition, it's important that the United States provide nationwide support for parents, in the form of paid leave and job protection, during the last month of pregnancy. Without this benefit, many mothers are forced to work up until the last day or a few days before they deliver, in order to protect their jobs, make as much money as they can before leaving, or save what little paid leave time they have to spend with their new babies.

Another support needed is an information campaign, integrated with the preconception campaign, that explores issues of pregnancy. Many nations have active pregnancy health education campaigns that can serve as models. A public education campaign in France, for example, led to all alcoholic products being tagged with the "zero alcohol during pregnancy" label shown in Figure 3.4.

If the United States implemented the supports proposed in this chapter for both preconception and pregnancy health, we as a nation could make dramatic progress toward assuring the healthy development of fetuses. Offering these supports at the beginning of a fetus's brain development would play a powerful role in building a foundation for future brain development. This period of life is a perfect time to positively affect development. "When a woman becomes

Figure 3.4. "Zero Alcohol During Pregnancy" Label on French Alcoholic Products

Zéro alcool
pendant la grossesse

Source: Legislation and National Strategies, 2011

pregnant, whether she's 14 or 40, there's this window of opportunity," explains one practitioner, a nurse for 28 years who has worked with more than 150 mothers in the Nurse-Family Partnership model over the past 7 years. "They want to do what's right. They want to change bad behaviors, tobacco, alcohol, using a seat belt, anything" (Bornstein, 2012).

While it may seem costly, the provision of these supports is a wise investment. (For further discussion of this point, see Chapter 8). If support efforts are focused on the period when the brain is being built and is most plastic and adaptable—rather than later in life, when such efforts would require restructuring of the brain—these supports have a better chance of making a positive difference. Children cannot be expected to develop into fully functioning, competent adults if we don't provide them with a supported path for their development. By providing support for embryonic and fetal development, we can make the most cost-effective investment that is possible.

CHAPTER 4

What a Newborn Needs from Birth to 9 Months
The Bonding Period

Attachment to a baby is a long-term process, not a single, magical moment. The opportunity for bonding at birth may be compared to falling in love—staying in love takes longer and demands more work.

—Dr. T. Berry Brazelton, *Touchpoints*

Over the years, science has taught us a lot about babies' lives during their first few months. We now know that babies are curious, motivated learners from birth, not at all the "blooming buzzing confusion" described by William James or the "blank slates" of 1960s behaviorists. Nor are babies as oblivious of their surroundings as many people think (Pinker, 2003). They are born paying attention and are able to perceive differences in their experiences and learn from those experiences. They come into the world with skills and expectations. They can identify one object from another, see objects as separate functional units, and expect objects to operate in predictable ways and are startled when they don't. They can also estimate quantities, and use geometric cues to orient themselves in space (Landau & Spelke, 1988).

Although the majority of babies' brain cells form while still in the womb, the complex process of connecting and pruning synapses that begins during that time undergoes changes once the baby is born, becoming more dependent on experience. From birth forward, experiences and interactions with caregivers greatly influence whether babies' brains are stimulated or stunted. Pediatric neurologist Harry Chugani, who studies early brain development, notes, "There is no doubt that experience molds the young brain. The early years determine how the brain turns out—these are the years when we create the promise of a child's future. This is when we set the mold" (Schore, 2001a, p. 1).

The most important aspect of brain growth during this period is building and learning from relationships, for which babies are preprogrammed. Part of this preprogramming is expecting that familiar adults will be available and will care for them. This preprogramming is so specific that young babies are drawn to and seek out people with speech patterns that sound like the speech they heard while in the womb and soon after. As well as the specific people—for example, their mothers and other family members—they heard while in the womb, it also extends to an inclination to attend more to and be more interested in forming relationships when interacting with, people who share a familiar language and accent with the people they heard in the womb. Conversely, babies are less interested in seeking out attention from people they've interacted with if those people speak a foreign language or have an unfamiliar accent (Kinzler, Shutts, DeJesus, & Spelke, 2009). For the infant, this is simply a matter of survival. Being wired to prefer familiarity increases the probability of the baby bonding with the people most likely to have an investment in caring for him or her and remaining close. Creating secure, mutual bonds ensures that babies will survive and grow to be educated regarding their role in the family and culture of their birth. The information babies pick up from their relationships with caregivers structurally develops their young brains through the ongoing processing of their experiences and interactions (Nagy, 2011).

Seeing brain growth in infancy as just as much of a social process as it is a physical process is key to understanding babies' needs after birth—particularly why it's so important that the people who are going to be responsible for babies' long-term care are with them during the early months. Caregivers need to not only be present, but also provide womb-like safety for the critical second gestational period of brain growth and development. It's this social womb, previously discussed in Chapter 2, that protects and provides growth experiences for the young brain throughout the first 30 months of life.

THE SOCIAL WOMB, PART 1: THE TIME OF BONDING

As previously discussed, a baby's brain begins to structure itself through simple interactions right from birth. The creation of the social womb begins with these interactions, through which primary attachments are formed with a significant few people who will be committed enough to provide the safe, stable environment in which the baby will be protected and able to learn. For example, when a baby cries instinctually, the crying creates feelings in the caregiver and alerts the caregiver to the baby's distress; then the adult provides the anticipated attention or doesn't. After a few interactions, the baby quickly learns things such as the intensity of the cry needed to get that particular adult's attention. Through back-and-forth information exchange, children's brain architecture becomes structured, and children begin to expect certain responses from their caregivers. Gradually, they begin to build understanding of whether the adults they interact with can be trusted to provide for their needs. Whether or not the available caregivers are trustworthy, children use caregiving relationships to provide them with the experiences that they use for the development of their brains and the building of their minds (i.e., the way they come to perceive things based on early experience and subsequent expectation). As Jeree Pawl, past president of ZERO TO THREE, notes: "We are *mirrors* for a baby that tell him who he is. We are also *windows* that let him know what he can expect" (Pawl, 2011).

Babies' Need for Caring Interactions

This stage of development is a time in which babies' brains are incredibly receptive to the treatment and messages of others. Their nervous systems are designed to receive information through receptors throughout the body, based on the give-and-take of interactions between caregiver and baby. According to what a baby's physiological experience is, his or her brain is wired to cope with an anticipated future. For one baby, based on previous experience, a smile could mean that a soft caress is coming; for another, a smile could mean that sometimes a slap is on the way. How children react to a new experience is emotionally, intellectually, and physically processed, and the meaning of that experience is deduced based on what has been gleaned from similar past experiences.

What babies need at this period of development is caring and predictable interactions in a social setting in which the brain can develop. Both tender, loving care and pertinent information essential to personal survival are instinctively sought out by babies. Help with babies' survival must start early. As one of our parent interviewees commented, this can be a scary time:

> The first night that you're home you're kind of bewildered, going, "I thank God they let us bring this little tiny fragile thing home." Like I have to take this enormous test to pass to get my driver's license, and here I am; they just give me this thing and assume I'm going to be feeding it.

The need of the baby to be protected is particularly acute immediately after birth. The first 28 days of life is a vulnerable period, as babies enlist their newly created bodies to help them make the transition from an intrauterine existence to an independent one (Nagy, 2011). Some babies don't survive the transition; generally the worst outcomes fall on those who have been exposed to risk factors while in the womb or whose mothers didn't receive prenatal care. In the United States significant disparities exist in neonatal mortality among various populations: the mortality rate among African Americans is 8.92 per thousand live births, while among non-Hispanic Whites it is 3.71 per thousand live births. As discussed in Chapter 3, this is due in part to both prenatal and perinatal risk factors that need to be addressed before and during pregnancy. It is also often due to a lack of well-baby care right after birth, which is why the American Academy of Pediatrics (AAP) (2008) recommends that all babies have neonatal visits to their primary medical home within 3 to 5 days after birth and again by 1 month of age. Additionally, most developed nations provide all babies with either in-home or doctor's-office wellness care. This is not the case in the United States.

Neonatal mortality is also linked to parents' ability to be present and care for their infants rather than having to be at work. Ruhm's (2000) study of 16 European nations between 1969 and 1994 demonstrated positive associations between paid parental-leave entitlements and reductions in infant and young-child mortality, with the largest decreases occurring in postneonatal deaths at between 2 and 12 months. A study by Tanaka (2005) found that paid-leave rights had a similarly positive effect on reducing low-weight births. Yet the United States has yet to enact a national parental paid-leave policy.

Thankfully, most babies do make it past the first 28 days. However, they then immediately face another developmental hurdle: the forming of relationships between themselves and their caregivers. The first few months can be very confusing for parents as they get the hang of taking care of their babies and dealing with fears that they will do something wrong. At the same time, babies are dealing with a genetically programmed "unfinishedness" that needs these relationships to nurture their bodies and brains. Evidence of this purposeful unfinishedness is the overlapping of the skull bones during the birth process and the space that is left for additional brain growth after the baby is born.

Babies' Remarkable Skills and Abilities

While babies' physical development is incomplete, they already have skills and abilities that prepare them to play an active role in their development. Early on, they use these skills to orient themselves to those caregivers whom they prefer and use built-in implicit memory (i.e., not requiring conscious processing) to encode their brains' experiences and use that encoding to create expectations for the future and for interpreting and learning about the world (Siegel, 1999). Foremost among these skills, the ability to discriminate through sounds, smells, tastes, and touches is present at birth and is a way of identifying and connecting with trusted others. Babies show clear preferences for their mothers' heartbeat and voice over those of strangers (Kisilevsky et al., 2003).

Almost immediately after birth, babies exhibit a remarkable social competence. They orient to objects and track them and, by 4 weeks of age, demonstrate a preference for looking at human faces over objects. They are biologically programmed to build relationships and to get people to love them enough to take care of them (DeCasper & Fifer, 1980).

Rather than being a passive recipient of care, babies actively elicit it. They respond to those around them in ways that elicit interest and increase the likelihood of continued contact and closeness (Marvin & Britner, 2008). This built-in way of relating to those around them actually keeps them alive. First, they differentiate one adult from another, and then, based on the feedback they get from early exchanges, they direct their attachment behaviors toward developing secure relationships with their primary caregivers. You can witness a magical dance taking place between babies as young as 6 weeks of age and their caregivers—exchanges that resemble conversations in the back-and-forth of timing and sequencing of the sounds, gestures, and facial expressions. It almost looks as though the baby is wooing the adult. These "conversations" are a significant part of the attachment process. What babies and adults are doing through these playful exchanges is getting to know each other. By the time babies are 12 weeks old, patterns of caregiver/baby interaction are being filed in their brains, allowing them to develop expectations as they come to learn whether they can or cannot depend on adults and to adjust their behaviors accordingly.

Because young infants can't physically move to adults, it's important that caregivers make themselves available and stay close in the early stages of this relating process. Adults need to take responsibility for ensuring closeness: listening for messages from the baby, providing for the baby's physical needs, and keeping the baby out of harm's way (Marvin & Britner, 2008). Research has shown that building strong baby/caregiver relationships depends on a particular type of caregiving behavior, including sensitivity to the needs and messages of the baby, timeliness in responding to those messages (particularly messages of distress), accurate reading of a child's cues, and the provision of appropriate levels of stimulation (Belsky & Fearon, 2008). Think of what types of care many babies are not getting during this early time period if their caregiving parents are already back at work and their caregivers are constantly changing, as often happens in child care.

SUPPORTS NECESSARY TO SUSTAIN DEVELOPMENT DURING THE FIRST 9 MONTHS OF LIFE

As previously discussed, babies' development from birth through their first 9 months is best served by their spending their days in the presence of close family members who live with them, who are emotionally and physically available to them, and with whom they can form primary attachments. It is also well served by their spending time with interested, available, and qualified extended family members and non-family members with whom they can form secondary attachments. Of great importance is the baby and the baby's family having early contact with a trained child-development professional who can identify early developmental delays or behavioral concerns in the child, recommend appropriate interventions, and help parents with issues related to early parenting, such as breastfeeding, responding to a baby's cry, and sleep issues. This help should start as early as possible, even in the hospital. For example, Klaus, Kennell, and Klaus (1995) found that mothers who nursed their infants during the first 3 hours after birth and then spent more than 15 hours with them over the next 3 days displayed greater emotional attraction to their infants 1 month later, compared to mothers with minimal postpartum contact. This points to the importance of the right assistance happening at the right time. It is also critical to the baby's health, development, and physical well-being that, early on, a child-development professional observes how the baby is being parented, so that abuse, neglect, a parent's mental illness or inappropriate feeding, handling, and sleep practices can be identified and addressed with early intervention. What babies need in these early months are time and opportunities for many emotionally rich interactions with trusted caregivers, and speedy intervention when these interactions don't happen.

When primary caregivers are anxious, depressed, preoccupied with non-child-related issues, or unsure of their ability to care for a child, they're often unable to provide the responsive type of care the child seeks. For example, researchers have shown that depressed mothers tend to be less responsive, more negative, and emotionally more subdued during social play with their infants. Their children, as early as 2 to 3 months of age, reflected this diminished responsiveness and animation even during interactions with nondepressed strangers (Thompson & Meyer, 2007). The social supports available to parents can also contribute to children's abilities to develop secure attachments. Parents with more support tend to be more responsive and sensitive when interacting with their children than parents who are socially isolated or lacking support.

Providing Comprehensive Well-Baby Care

The ideal context for care in babies' first 9 months is best ensured by providing the health coverage recommended in Chapter 3 for families of all incomes, and including necessary inoculations, well-baby care visits, developmental screening, and affordable intervention services if needed. Since 1967, it has been the position of the American Academy of Pediatrics that parental assistance during these early months is critical. For example, in the area of well-baby care, the AAP recommends six well-baby care visits before the 12th month, in addition to a newborn visit and a follow-up visit 4 or 5 days after leaving the hospital. This assistance could ensure a young baby's adequate weight gain, identify and address mental-health issues, confirm or perform recommended newborn screenings, and address parent concerns (Council on Pediatric Practice, 1967).

In a randomized study, Casey and Whitt (1980) assigned mothers to receive either standard well-child care or enhanced well-child care designed to promote mother/child interaction in the first 6 months of life. The enhanced care included counseling to promote understanding of normal child development and awareness of the social nature of infant behaviors, as well as encouragement for increasing mothers' responsiveness and understanding of their infants' individuality. Mothers in the enhanced-care group rated significantly higher on sensitivity, cooperation, appropriateness of interaction, and play than did the control group who received standard well-child care.

Many countries around the world provide this kind of assistance to all families as a matter of course (Kuo et al., 2006). For example, in the state of Victoria, Australia, home visits are provided to every home with a new baby 7 to 10 days after the baby is born, with follow-up visits at 2 weeks, 4 weeks, 8 weeks, 4 months, 8 months, 12 months, 18 months, and 2 years. This service has been provided to all Victorian families since 1920—in addition to an Australian national policy of 12 months of paid parental leave—and is part and parcel of Victorian family life. One of the nurse practitioners who provide this service in Victoria reported that the use of this service greatly increased the continuation of breastfeeding, helped family members tune in to the temperaments and cues sent by babies, and provided an avenue for the treatment of postpartum and extended depression (Hatton, Harrison-Hohner, Coste, Dorato, Curet, & McCarron, 2005).

What we find in the United States is that the combined absence of paid parental leave and well-baby visits leads to the cessation of breastfeeding and the onset or provocation of depression, which interferes with, among other things, secure attachments and the structural development of the baby's brain. This can be quite harmful to development. Here is the experience of one mother interviewed:

> I was not as responsive to his [my baby's] cues and to language. I was having problems even feeding myself and making sure that I was eating enough. My nutrition wasn't great, and that could have an impact on him to a certain extent, but even more on me, 'cause if you're not eating well during pregnancy and nursing . . . that has an overall long-term impact.

Diagnosing and Treating Depression in Mothers

Field (1992) found that, in a sample of depressed mothers, 70% appeared to have chronic depression that persisted across the first 6 months of the infant's life. The infants of these mothers showed delays in growth and development at 12 months. According to Field (1998), infants of depressed mothers are negatively affected by the depression as early as the neonatal period. By 6 months, this dysregulation is characterized by limited responsivity to adults, excessive sleep, elevated norepinephrine and cortisol levels, and limited responsivity to facial expressions. Neurological delays are also found at this age. At 9 months fewer social references are found in children with depressed mothers than non-depressed mothers, and at 12 months play and exploratory behavior are more limited for the children of depressed mothers. In a more recent study, Chatterji and Markowitz (2008) focused on depression as a maternal health outcome because clinical depression and self-reported depressive symptoms among mothers put children, particularly in the early years, at risk of adverse emotional and cognitive development. In one of their studies, maternal depression was measured by a widely used psychiatric scale that captures mood, sleeping problems, and motor functioning level. On the basis of results from this scale, doubling total maternity leave for a relatively brief amount of time—from 9 to 18 weeks—was estimated to reduce maternal depressive symptoms by a small but significant amount.

Screening was also crucial to uncover postpartum depression because most new mothers do not recognize their problem as depression (Seidman, 1998). Twenty-five percent of cases of severe postpartum depression become chronic, with delayed treatment being the greatest factor in the development of chronic depression (Forman, Videbech, Hedegaard, Dalby, & Secher, 2000).

With regard to the cause of some of this depression, one interviewed mother comments:

> I would say that I've been feeling depressed. After giving birth and at my six-week check-up, they asked me if I'm feeling sad or is your mood low? At that time? No, not really. I was feeling fine. It's only been in the past week or so [before going back to work] it's really come to the realization that I'm going back to work that I've been feeling depressed. I've cried several times a day about having to go back and having to leave her . . . It surprises me how strong the emotion is. I knew it would be difficult [to go back to work] and I would be sad about it . . . but it surprises me how strong that feeling is . . . It's the need that she has for me . . . it's just a biological need. There's no substitute that you can make for that.

Another mother says that even her doctor didn't pick up on her depression:

> The doctor would generally ask me, "Oh, how are you doing?" in a very open way. You know, "are you doing okay?" Maybe that was her idea of starting a conversation about if I was having an issue of depression. It's not like you wake up one day and suddenly you're depressed . . . There

was an online kind of like mom pregnancy community, and there are different conversations, and so I was talking online with all these other women that had been diagnosed with postpartum depression, that I was able to recognize the symptoms. But my doctor never brought it up.

It is particularly important to diagnose and treat depression early because many new mothers experience it. "Baby blues," the most common mood disturbance after childbirth, may affect nearly 50% of new mothers, and 10% to 15% of mothers suffer from clinical depression after pregnancy (Evans, Heron, Francomb, Oke, & Golding, 2001). A recent estimate suggests that as many as 17% of women with young children have elevated levels of depressive symptoms, and that these symptoms are likely to persist throughout the child's preschool years (Horwitz, Briggs-Gowan, Storfer-Isser, & Carter, 2009). Additionally, thoughts of harming infants are more frequent among depressed mothers. In one sample, 41% of depressed mothers, compared to 7% of control-group mothers, admitted to thoughts of harming their infants. More than half of the depressed mothers had problems with thoughts of harming their infants, fear of being alone with the infants, and an inability to care for the infants (Jennings, Ross, Popper, & Elmore, 1999). We now know that infants as young as 3 months of age are able to detect depression in their mothers, which may potentially compromise their social, emotional, and cognitive functioning (Weinberg & Tronick, 1998), so early detection and treatment is key.

Recognizing the Importance of Breastfeeding

With regard to the ongoing importance of breastfeeding, the AAP and the World Health Organization recommend that babies be exclusively breastfed for at least 6 months and transitioned to non-exclusive breastfeeding at least through 9 months (American Academy of Pediatrics, 2012; World Health Organization, 2012). However, in the United States, two-thirds of mothers surveyed by the U.S. Department of Health and Human Services did not breastfeed for as long as they'd intended, whether 1 month, 6 months, or longer. In the United States, while 75% of mothers start out breastfeeding, only 13% of babies are exclusively breastfed at the end of 6 months (U.S. Department of Health and Human Services, 2011a).

As with other issues, support from pediatricians and nurses during the postpartum hospitalization and postdischarge periods is crucial for breastfeeding continuation. On January 20, 2011, U.S. Surgeon General Regina M. Benjamin issued a general "Call to Action to support breast-feeding," outlining steps that can be taken to remove some of the obstacles faced by women who want to breastfeed their babies. "Many barriers exist for mothers who want to breast-feed," Dr. Benjamin said. "They shouldn't have to go it alone. Whether you're a clinician, a family member, a friend, or an employer, you can play an important part in helping mothers who want to breastfeed" (U.S. Department of Health and Human Services, 2011b).

Bettina Forbes, co-founder of Best for Babes, makes a more specific recommendation: "If every expecting mother were seen by a board-certified lactation consultant that can help her set goals appropriate for her situation, and work with her to develop a plan to overcome any barriers along the way, breastfeeding rates would skyrocket, and we would all benefit" (Rochman, 2012).

It has been well documented that the presence or absence of paid leave also has a powerful impact on the duration of breastfeeding. In 2006, while three-fourths of new mothers in the United States started breastfeeding, only one-third continued to breastfeed their babies exclusively for 3 months, and only 14% breastfed exclusively for 6 months (Centers for Disease Control and Prevention, 2011a). It was reported that the main reason so many women stopped breastfeeding early was that they had to return to work. Many new mothers find it difficult to continue breastfeeding because of conditions at work. A survey by the National Women's Health Resource Center (2007) reported that 32% of new mothers give up breastfeeding fewer than 7 weeks after returning to work because of significant barriers to breastfeeding in the workplace. The most significant barriers included

- lack of privacy;
- inflexible work schedules;
- lack of refrigeration to store breast milk; and
- insufficient or nonexistent company policies to allow them to take an adequate number of breaks to pump.

Currently, only 11 states have laws facilitating breastfeeding at work (National Women's Health Resource Center, 2007). This lack of support for breastfeeding on the job, combined with a widespread lack of paid parental leave, stacks the deck against new U.S. mothers' continuing breastfeeding for at least the 6 months recommended by the AAP. For example, a British study found that the longer a mother delayed her return to work, the more likely she was to breastfeed for at least 4 months (Hawkins et al., 2007). Other studies have found a high incidence of breastfeeding discontinuation in mothers who lack support from family and friends, have insufficient breastfeeding education, and return to work full time shortly after giving birth (Losch, Dungy, Russell, & Dusdieker, 1995; Piper & Parks, 1996). As can be seen from the testimony of a mother interviewed for this book, ending breastfeeding early can be hard on both mother and child:

> I really don't know how to leave my baby. Even though she's had a bottle once a day pretty much since she was a week old, she doesn't always take the bottle very well, and she'll get hysterical, crying so hard, she can hardly catch her breath. It's very difficult to calm her down, and the only way, oftentimes, she will calm down is for me to nurse her. It breaks my heart because her mother is going to be taken away from her and she doesn't understand that. She has no capacity to understand that.

Another reason for abandoning breastfeeding early is mothers' difficulty with successfully and nonpainfully conducting the physical act of breastfeeding. In countries where well-baby care is practiced, assistance with breastfeeding, to help mothers continue the practice, is commonly a major component of care. In the United States—whether because mothers have to return to work earlier, because mothers didn't receive assistance in successfully mastering the breastfeeding process, or due to other reasons—the percentage of mothers breastfeeding is much smaller than in countries with national paid leave and well-baby care policies (Lindberg, 1996; Tanaka, 2005; Winegarden & Bracy, 1995).

Unsurprisingly, a connection has been found between depression and cessation of breastfeeding. Early cessation of breastfeeding has been shown to lead to postnatal depression (Cooper, Murray, & Stein, 1993; Falceto, Giugliani, & Fernandes, 2004). The converse is also true: Henderson et al. (2003) found that postpartum depression has a significantly negative effect on breastfeeding duration, and Tavares, Drevets, and Sahakian (2003) have shown that mothers with higher depressive-symptom scores were more likely to discontinue breastfeeding at 12 weeks than mothers without symptoms. Other studies have shown that postpartum depressive symptomology of mothers predicted a reduced preference for breastfeeding at later ages (Cooper et al., 1993; Galler, Harrison, Biggs, Ramsey, & Forde, 1999).

HOW U.S. POLICIES NEGATIVELY IMPACT BABIES

Breastfeeding cessation and depression are just two of the many negative parental conditions that can be positively influenced by paid parental leave and well-baby care. This is why many countries make an investment in having primary caregivers and babies spend time together during the baby's first year of life, and provide professional support for them to do so during the early months. These countries see it as a "pay now or pay later" proposition.

Interruption in the Bonding Process

Of 173 nations, including all of the United States' major economic competitors and many far-less-affluent nations, the United States is joined by only three others—Liberia, Papua New Guinea, and Swaziland—in not providing nationwide paid parental leave for mothers in any segment of the workforce (Heymann, Earle, & Hayes, 2007). This makes the United States the only advanced industrialized nation that does not provide some wage replacement for primary caregivers to stay home and care for a new baby.

Thus, just as U.S. parents are in the middle of this "getting to know each other" process, figuring out and bonding with their new children, they have to return to work. It's becoming routine to interrupt the bonding process, as mothers often return to work just weeks after delivery. Four times as many first-time mothers in the United States as in the United Kingdom return to work by the time their child is 2 months old (Washbrook, Ruhm, Waldfogel, & Han, 2011). Nearly 60% of all new U.S. mothers are back at work—the majority, full time—9 months after giving birth, compared to only 20% of their Canadian counterparts (Han, Ruhm, Waldfogel, & Washbrook, 2008). Between 1991 and 1994, 13% of U.S. first-time mothers who were employed during pregnancy had returned to work by 1 month after childbirth. The number returning by 2 months after childbirth rose to 30%; the number returning by 3 months after childbirth was 41%. Within a year, 76% of first-time mothers were back in the workforce (Smith, Downs, & O'Connell, 2011).

U.S. parents are putting their children in child care at much earlier ages than parents in other countries. Given that we are the only industrialized nation that does not provide a national paid-leave policy, we shouldn't be surprised at this rush back to work. For many of the U.S. working poor, it's an act almost mandated by the government. As a result of welfare-reform legislation enacted in 1996, many states make returning to work as early as 3 months after the birth of a child a condition for the continued receipt of cash assistance.

Concerns About Interactions in Child Care

The caregiver/baby interactional process described in this chapter occurs with other caregivers as well as with family members. When parents put children, particularly young infants, into child care, it's important to remember that the children's attachment interactions in a child-care environment are similar to those that occur within the home: in the absence of their primary caregiver, they'll seek out those in the child-care setting who show a willingness to form emotional relationships and set about developing secure and trusting relationships with them. Although this attachment doesn't need to have the same intensity as those between babies and their primary caregivers, emotional connection is crucial. It is this emotional connection that serves as the base for learning.

By approximately 6 months of age, infants can read the facial and vocal expressions of their caregivers and mentally process those readings. It's at this point that children start to understand the internal experiences, thoughts, and motives of others; this understanding, in turn, is used to build cognitive skills, develop notions of self, and begin to make connections between one's own and other people's feelings (Thompson & Meyer, 2007). The loving support and stimulating experiences provided by caregivers lead children to function better, both in the moment and later in life (Calkins & Hill, 2007). Over time, infants learn from the strategies used by their caregivers and integrate them into their own ways of behaving, leading to, among other things, the development of social competence, self-understanding, the growth of conscience, and moral awareness (Thompson, 2011, p. 14). This is why it's so important for both in-home and out-of-home relationships to be solid. As discussed in Chapter 5, the likelihood of that happening is not high without adequate support. Those providing infant/toddler care may not always be the best models or may not be in the baby's life long enough for the baby to establish and benefit from a relationship.

Insufficient Well-Baby Care

As with paid parental leave, other countries see the value of well-baby care for both improving parenting practices and addressing developmental delays. These countries understand that lack of well-baby care increases the likelihood of preventable hospitalization among high-risk or chronically ill children and places infants who survive a preterm birth at greater risk of developing both short- and long-term health complications. Additionally, many debilitating effects of health issues, including cerebral palsy, sensory and motor disabilities, respiratory illnesses, and learning and behavioral disorders, can be prevented with well-baby care. Therefore, most European countries provide home visitation services or regular well-baby clinic visits for newborns and their families. In the United States, where home visitation services are provided to just a fraction of families—mainly to members of at-risk populations who qualify for social services—most children don't receive services until there is an emergency. One new mother interviewed for this book speaks about the need to provide these services:

> I think, for parents to be really who they want to be as parents and to feel competent in being at home with their children, they really do need the well-baby visits or the support in place so that they can feel competent in that new role.

Compared to children whose well-baby care is up-to-date, children with insufficient well-baby care (the majority of children) are more likely to visit a hospital emergency room (Mustin, Holt, & Connell, 1994). Lives can be saved if well-baby care services are provided for all babies in the United States. In 2003, 8.9% of infant deaths that occurred after the perinatal period and were not associated with congenital abnormalities were the result of infectious, endocrine, nutritional, or metabolic diseases (Hoyert, Kung, & Smith, 2005). Most well-baby home visits include screenings for most such diseases, as well as routine physical examinations that aid early diagnosis and treatment. In some cases, needed treatment can be as simple as administering vitamin supplements and maintaining routine follow-up care; in others, readily available vaccines could be recommended for many infectious diseases.

National Accountability

The impact of not having a national paid-leave program and universal well-baby care, screening, and follow-up services in the United States is creating a significant barrier to the development of young babies. If one missing support doesn't get them another will. This was bad treatment of babies even before we understood that young brains depended on the attachments they formed in their first 9 months to provide them with necessary experiences. Given what we have learned about the important structuring of the brain that occurs during this period, it is foolhardy to withhold necessary services from babies. Without these support services, the chances of babies' brains getting through this period of development unscathed are greatly diminished. If we as a nation ignore the new information that science has provided us about the needs of the young brain, and continue to withhold help to families during the critical first 9 months of babies' lives, the neglect will be purposeful.

CHAPTER 5

What the Infant Needs from 7 to 18 Months

The Exploration Stage

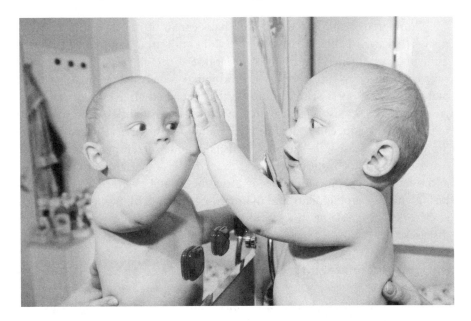

Allow the child to be authentic, to move, to feel the way they move, appreciating them for what they are.

—Magda Gerber

As babies reach their seventh month, they enter a second stage of experience-influenced brain development, during which their efforts become more coordinated, purposeful, and social in nature. With increasing physical competence, they gain greater independent movement. They are also developing more sophisticated ways of signaling their needs. This means that babies have the ability to physically act on choices, approaching or distancing themselves from people and stimuli, and when in need of comfort, a baby in this stage may crawl to and reach for an adult while giving a vocal message to express his or her desire to be held, rather than just crying. In a few short months, babies have developed better attention capacity, motor control, and self-regulation, allowing them to examine and relate to objects and people more thoroughly (Calkins & Hill, 2007; Eisenberg, Hofer, & Vaughan, 2007).

THE SOCIAL WOMB, PART 2:
THE TIME OF EXPLORATION

As they begin the exploration stage, babies exert greater energy in experimenting with their new physical skills and show more curiosity for examining the enticing objects and people around them. These new skills and interests mean that babies are making many independent choices about interactions with caregivers and their environment, but the independence of freedom of movement and the drive for exploration are often in conflict with the continued need for the safety and security caregivers provide. It's common to see babies in motion throughout the day, repeatedly setting out on "adventures" in their environment, returning to the "home base" that their caregivers provide, and then leaving again. Now that they have the ability to "hold" their caregivers in mind for a while (Pawl, 2006), this cycle of moving away for self-interest and returning for support and connection teaches babies a great deal about how to separate and stay connected. While not yet truly independent, they are practicing for their future independence. Even as they distance themselves from caregivers and seemingly become absorbed in exploring an object or mastering a skill, they do a lot of "checking in," looking at their caregivers from afar to see if the caregiver is watching and acknowledging their efforts. These early interactions around exploration impact children's sense of security in engaging the ever-expanding world around them, building new brain structures as babies work to both explore new things and stay connected.

An Expanded Learning Agenda

While the experiences of the first few months of life have already impacted brain development, a new kind of programming begins during the exploration stage. Based on adults' reactions to children's acts of dependent and independent functioning, children are gaining an understanding of which independent explorations are socially appropriate and which dangers they should avoid in the environment, from the point of view of their caregivers. As they learn about what they are and are not allowed to explore, they also begin to understand what types of help they can expect in exploring and whether or not certain caregivers will be available to offer support when solo exploration becomes frightening. The brain is preparing for life that doesn't revolve entirely around caregiver support, a time when, for example, children will have to use the lessons they've learned from caregivers to independently identify risks like a poisonous berry on a bush or an ungated stairway. They are learning lessons that will serve them well later on in life, when the caregiver will not be there to assist them in handling those dangers.

Even as they try to assert independence, babies will enlist their caregivers for joint exploration. Babies can learn many lessons by observing and imitating the caregivers' actions. They also begin to understand how they can use their caregivers to help them pursue their own goals and facilitate their learning.

Mirror Neurons:
Another Form of Connection with Others

We are preprogrammed to learn from those who care for us; our inborn gene and neuron systems wait to be activated by experience. While watching and interacting with other people, sets of neurons cluster, fire, and eventually wire together to help babies to react and respond appropriately to similar future events, even in a caregiver's absence.

The existence of mirror neurons was only recently discovered, shedding more light on how we learn from others (Gallese, 2001). Mirror neuron systems are systems that have been hardwired in our brains to detect patterns of movement that predict future movement (e.g., a hand holding food and moving up toward the face is presumed to be going to the mouth). This helps babies, even at an early age, to "read the minds" of others, predicting intentions based on movement. Watching others act sets off babies' mirror neurons. As these neurons fire, babies experience some of the same physical sensations as the person they are observing does. This means that seeing someone in pain can cause pain, but it also means that even young babies can calculate others' intentions. Mirror neurons help babies both anticipate the outcome of a movement and mirror the mental state (e.g., relaxed, alert) of those with whom they are interacting for better attunement.

The discovery of mirror neurons means we now know that babies take in and learn from much more input than was ever previously thought possible (Gallese, 2001). It's important to note, however, that a baby is clearly not a "sponge," merely soaking up input from caregivers. Both babies and caregivers call forth, give, and receive messages, with babies just as capable of initiating interaction as caregivers. Driven by a built-in learning agenda, babies search out lessons on preprogrammed topics and learn.

WHAT BABIES NEED TO GET FROM RELATIONSHIPS

Just as potential neural connections are preprogrammed into the central nervous system, so are certain expectations for relationships. As pointed out earlier, babies are born expecting to receive treatment from adults that ensures and increases the possibility of their survival. More specifically, from first contact with the world outside the womb, babies want adults to protect and nurture them, read their messages without distortion, and give them clear, appropriately responsive messages. The extent to which adults meet these expectations in interacting with babies determines how babies organize their emotional security around those adults (Thompson, Thompson, & Luckenbill, 2011).

In the exploration stage, babies handle and process more information of greater complexity, while still relying on the safety of the social womb. Their interactions with adults begin to prepare them for successful functioning in society, and, through observation and exploration, they are already beginning to learn about the world that exists around them. During this stage, babies also start to use messages from caregivers to develop perceptions of self, forming perceptions of whether they are lovable or unlovable based on how caregivers have responded to them up to this point and developing internal working models for how to engage others based on these perceptions. They also use their perceptions of how their caregivers treat them to generalize about expected behaviors of unfamiliar adults. Providing secure, trusting relationships and responsive interactions helps infants and young toddlers develop better feelings about themselves, more positive expectations for the behaviors of others, and improved social skills and understanding; thus, these young children are better enabled to relate smoothly with people new to them and to engage in play with peers (Schore, 2001b). Positive interactions with caregivers also give young children confidence in their newly developing skills and motivation to continue to explore the world and make discoveries (Bowlby,

1985). Conversely, experiencing stressful interactions on a regular basis can damage children's brain development and their ability to develop future relationships (Schore, 2000). This brings into stark focus why the competency and mental health of those who care for babies during the early months of life must be considered of highest importance. Whether at home or in child care, adults directly influence the person a baby becomes.

A Base for Learning

The attachment relationships that began forming immediately after birth continue into the exploration stage. Bowlby (1982) describes babies' basic question during exploration as "Is my attachment figure nearby, available, and able to attend to my needs?" If children perceive the answer to be yes, they tend to feel relaxed, confident, and safe and are therefore more likely to interact with others, play with peers, and engage in and share discoveries. However, children who fear that their caregivers will be unavailable tend to be more anxious to search for the caregiver, cry, or experience distress.

Among the important lessons children learn at this phase of development is a beginning understanding of socially appropriate ways to express emotions. Whether through intentional choice or not, parents and other caregivers shape the day-to-day emotional climate that babies experience. Their methods of expressing their emotions and responding to situations act to socialize children into understanding which emotions are appropriate to express in various situations and how vociferous they can be in expressing themselves (Denham, 1998).

Attachment relationships are not just vital for sound emotional development; they form the foundation for growth in all developmental domains, broadening physical, social, intellectual, and communicative horizons. If babies have already established secure attachment relationships, they'll find it easier to engage in complex and expanding give-and-take interactions with their caregivers and others. As they move further into the world, their caregivers become more than just a source for having their basic needs met; they become interpreters through whom babies can better understand the expanding world around them. Through shared experiences—whether initiated by caregivers or themselves—babies learn about new behaviors and objects, examining their caregivers for cues as to whether to engage in or avoid interactions or how to determine various objects' functions. Children at this age are more inclined to explore independently when their caregiver is in the vicinity and available to them. Researchers watching babies working from a base of secure attachment have described "secure exploration" as confident, attentive, eager, and resourceful exploration of materials or tasks, accompanied by persistence and the ability to tolerate moderate levels of frustration, in the pursuit of some goal (Grossmann, Grossman, Kindler, & Zimmermann, 2008).

The Learning of Empathy and Social Understanding

During this stage of development, with the help of mirror neuron system firings, children are starting to develop the capacity to understand and experience the emotional or psychological states of other people. By providing nurturing care to children and modeling caring interactions with others, caregivers support children's emerging empathy, social understanding, and prosocial behaviors (Quann & Wien, 2006). Babies come to understand what to expect from others, how to engage in back-and-forth social interactions, and different ways of acting in different social situations (Eisenberg, 2000; Zahn-Waxler & Radke-Yarrow, 1990). Additionally, babies' ability to assess their social surroundings is connected to how adults talk to them, as babies tend to demonstrate greater social understanding when their caregivers comment on the babies' own emotional experiences and mental states. When this starts at about 6 months of age and continues with developmentally appropriate "conversations" about desires, thoughts, knowledge, and the emotions of others, researchers see greater social understanding in babies who received this type of attention, compared to babies who didn't (Taumoepeau & Ruffman, 2008).

Growth of Communication Skills

The exploration stage coincides with a dramatic increase in a baby's communication skills and language comprehension. In the time between 7 months and 1 year of age, a child generally learns to say a few words and understand many more (Kopp, 2003); adult input is key to this learning. When adults speak with infants—communicating emotions, thoughts, and beliefs; sharing experiences; and conveying messages about cultural rules, family preferences, and appropriate ways of acting and feeling—it stimulates the development of language pathways in the brain and leads to a blossoming of linguistic knowledge even before infants can respond with words (Siegel, 1999; Thompson, 2011). It's not just the words that matter, but also the larger patterns of communication—not just what is said but how it is said, and how it is received (Pawl & John, 1995).

SUPPORTS NECESSARY TO SUSTAIN DEVELOPMENT
FROM 7 TO 18 MONTHS

Given the rapidity of brain growth during this period of development and the babies' acute sensitivity to experience, the following supports are necessary to ensure healthy brain development.

1. Continued Well-Baby Care. A primary ongoing support that babies need during this stage of life is continued well-baby care. Critical for babies' development are help with parenting; assessment of developmental delays and other difficulties, including parent health and mental health issues; and when necessary, intervention. Assistance for parents and children to get back on track when health or development gets derailed also should continue through this stage (Kuo et al., 2006).

At this stage, many families will need help navigating the transition of putting a baby into child care, a lifestyle change that can impact both the baby and other family members. The importance of ensuring time and opportunity for the continued development of secure, trusting relationships between babies and primary caregivers can't be overemphasized, and this should remain a goal of well-baby care visits, as should help with selecting care.

2. Availability of Affordable, High-Quality Infant/Toddler Care. Children's success depends on child care being both affordable and of the highest possible quality. When choosing a child-care provider, parents should seek out providers who will allow sufficient time and opportunity to establish and develop secure and trusting relationships with the children in their care. Parents should also receive some degree of assurance that these relationships will remain stable, rather than being severed due to employee turnover or other factors. The caregivers need to be knowledgeable enough about children's development to provide caring, responsive attention in an environment that provides safe, interesting, and developmentally appropriate opportunities to explore and learn.

3. Caregiver Access to Consulting Professionals. Finally, whether home- or center-based, child-care programs serving children during the exploration stage need to have access to consulting professionals who can provide guidance and ensure that caregivers receive help with issues of early childhood mental health, special education, and child development. This help will improve caregivers' ability to quickly identify developmental issues and recommend appropriate intervention services when necessary. Given the current low-quality level of care cited in numerous studies (as discussed in the following section), infant-care programs need help in identifying and alleviating both child-based and staff-based problems.

THE LOW QUALITY OF CHILD CARE IN THE UNITED STATES

Much to U.S. children's detriment, there are currently many obstacles standing in the way of providing all babies with the necessary quality level of care. A national study by the NICHD Early Child Care Research Network (2000) identified positive caregiving as a primary indicator of child-care quality. The study found that approximately 30% of children received a "fair" level of positive caregiving (on a scale that placed "fair" between "poor" and "good") across their first 3 years of life. Fewer than 10% of arrangements evaluated were rated as providing high-quality care.

Another study found that only 12% to 14% of children are in child-care arrangements that promote their growth and learning (Shore, 1997). Helburn and colleagues (Helburn, 1995) observed 401 centers in California, Colorado, Connecticut, and North Carolina that served infants, toddlers, and/or preschool-age children and found that only one in four infant classrooms met the "good" benchmarks as set by the *Infant/Toddler Environment Rating Scale (ITERS)* (Harms, Cryer, & Clifford, 1990). In a study (Howes, Phillips, & Whitebook, 1992) rating "Developmentally Appropriate Practices and Appropriate Caregiving," infant-toddler classrooms scored a 3.1 out of 7, compared to a score of 4 for classrooms serving preschool-age children on the same dimensions, on the *Early Childhood Environment Rating Scale (ECERS)* (Harms & Clifford, 1980).

Another team of researchers (Fuller, Kagan, Loeb, & Chang, 2004) observed the quality of 166 centers and 187 nonparental home settings serving children from low-income families in California, Connecticut, and Florida. They found that mothers working the most hours per week tended to select the lowest-quality home-based providers, meaning that the children of these mothers received a "double whammy": long hours away from close family and low-quality care. One mother interviewed for this book describes her unsettling experience with child care:

> [To locate child care], I got a 1-800 number, and they send you
> referrals. You call them and set up interviews. We found a child-care
> provider that would do it as in-home. I went and interviewed her for

probably an hour or two hours with our baby, and she seemed very nice. She had a few other kids there. It would be six total with them. He was there for probably five months before we decided to take him out because we noticed progressively that the house was dirtier. Every time we showed up to pick him up, he was just sitting in an ExerSaucer. It just seemed like she [the caregiver] was getting a little lazy. We found out that he was taking supposedly two-hour naps upstairs in a crib with no baby monitor. I mentioned something about getting a baby monitor and nothing was ever done. I would show up, and he was still in the crib, or he would be crying. So we eventually decided to take him out of that situation.

Skill Levels of Child-Care Providers

Low levels of training, certification, and credentialing limit quality of care for infants. Researchers at San Francisco State University's Marian Wright Edelman Institute found that more than half of San Francisco's 358 early childhood education providers operate at low to medium levels of quality (as assessed using the ECERS), indicating the need for more training. There is also significant evidence in support of increased certification and credentialing to counteract the exodus of professionals from the field. According to a recent report from the Foundation for Child Development, the proportion of center-based caregivers with at least a 4-year college degree dropped from 43% in 1983–1985 to 30% in 2002–2004, and new hires increasingly have only a high school degree or its equivalent. Among home-based providers, educational attainment levels were even lower, with more than 45% having a high school degree or less and only 11% having a 4-year college degree (Zigler, Marsland, & Lord, 2009). Researchers have noted the importance of teacher qualifications in raising the quality of child care (Barnett, 2003), and some have established a clear link between teacher qualifications and children's educational achievement (Bowman, Donovan, & Burns, 2000). Although not all experts agree, many have concluded that hiring teachers with a bachelor's degree in early childhood development or early childhood education is a key strategy for promoting high-quality child care (Whitebook & Bellm, 1999).

Compensation of Providers

One reason for the persistent poor quality of child care in the United States is our country's attitude toward the profession. Currently, in the United States, infant/toddler care is viewed as a low-status profession, and as little more than babysitting. As a program director interviewed for this book explained:

> [Caregivers] are working on a shoestring. They are trying to meet the emotional needs of babies and the demands of this challenging day, and yet they don't feel supported and resourced in a way that values the work that they are doing with babies every day.

Because of this prevailing attitude, infant/toddler care is often compensated at minimum wage. In many places, caregivers are paid less than locker-room attendants, bicycle repairers, and animal trainers. In 2004, infant/toddler–care providers earned an average of only $8.37 per hour, with half of them earning less than $7.90 per hour. The wages for early-child-care workers have not increased with inflation, averaging less than a 2% increase per year. Even more disturbing is that 25% of center-based caregivers and 35% of home-based caregivers have incomes below 200% of the poverty line, and these caregivers are often without supplementary benefits such as health insurance and pension plans. Recent data show that, among center-based caregivers, employer-provided health benefits and pensions are extended to only 33 and 21% of employees, respectively (Zigler, Marsland, & Lord, 2009). Yet, those providing infant/toddler care have one of the greatest teaching responsibilities in society, with a better possibility of influencing an individual's social development and learning potential than classroom teachers or university professors have. One child-care provider expressed frustration in this way:

> There is a very big difference between "taking care of babies" and providing high-quality early care and education, in a group setting, to children under one [year old]. The differences are apparent in measurable ways. . . . And yet, we continue to assume—through our policies and funding priorities—that infant development is automatic, and that those who work with them are not professionals . . . that they're not "teaching" anything. We also associate "good" teachers with natural and innate traits, which then reinforces the belief that they do not need specialized training, or compensation that matches their skills and education. I hold a B.A. in Child Development, an M.A. in ECE [Early Childhood Education]/Leadership, and have 10 years of ECE experience—but because I work with infants, I continue to earn less than the lowest-paid K–12 teachers in California.

Employee Turnover

Low compensation levels contribute to employee turnover, which the National Child Care Staffing Study found to have a detrimental impact on child-care quality and children's developmental outcomes. According to the California Early Care and Education Workforce Study, 15% of directors of San Francisco Bay Area child-care centers, as well as 18.1% of teachers and 22.3% of assistant teachers, left or stopped working during the previous year (California Child Care and Referral Network, 2006). These rates of employee turnover impede the quality, duration, and stability of the relationships children can form with their care providers. They also reflect a loss of skilled, experienced teachers from the field and require other staff to spend time filling in for missing teachers and training new colleagues.

Whitebook, Howes, and Phillips (1990) used observations and interviews to investigate the quality of 227 U.S. child-care centers in five major metropolitan areas. They reported an almost overwhelming annual turnover rate for early childhood teachers: 41%.

Care Environment

In addition to the variable skill levels and continuity of those providing child care, the environments in which the care takes place and the program policies and regulations under which the care is implemented have been found lacking throughout the country (National Association of Child Care Resource and Referral Agencies, 2006; Shore, 1997). *The NICHD Study of Early Child Care and Youth Development* (National Institute of Child Health and Human Development, 2006) found low quality scores related to practice guidelines in nonparental child-care settings. The study also found that child-care centers serving infants and toddlers were less likely to meet the American Academy of Pediatrics' recommended standards for adult-to-child ratios, group size, and staff education and training than were facilities serving preschool-age children.

Even the most highly qualified caregivers, however, will find it difficult to provide babies with the care they need while working under most states' weak child-care regulations. State regulations routinely ignore professional organizations' recommendations regarding ratio of adults to babies, total group size, amount of square feet available per child, continuity of child/caregiver relationships, and caregiver training and certification. (For example, see Appendix B for recommendations of the Program for Infant/Toddler Care [PITC].) Even when states have regulations and guidelines for child care, many states provide waivers exempting certain kinds of care providers from meeting established standards (National Association of Child Care Resource and Referral Agencies, 2011).

Sharing the Costs of High-Quality Care

The standards that high-quality child care must meet give it the potential to be a very expensive proposition. As one mother explained, "Day-care cost is extremely high here, and in order for me to afford it, I have to work while I go to school. And all of my money from work will go straight to day care, so I won't be making any money for the family." The costs of ensuring low caregiver-to-child ratios, small care groups, safe and interesting environments, and credentialed teachers can make it impossible for most parents to place their child in quality care and can drive care providers out of business. The solution in the United States, has been to offer lower-quality service.

European countries, on the other hand, have taken major steps to avoid this kind of compromise with quality. While U.S. families pay 80% of their child-care costs directly, that number is closer to 30% in Europe, with the remainder of the cost subsidized through various sources (Lally, 2010). Given the importance of this stage of life to a child's development, we must follow the European example and provide subsidies to ensure that child-care programs can afford to provide quality care and that parents can afford to place their children in it.

BABIES AT RISK

As discussed in this chapter, we've learned that in the period of life between 7 and 18 months of age, babies' relationships with caregivers serve as the foundation for learning. In these relationships, babies engage in communicative interactions that build their language skills; develop a preliminary social understanding of how to relate to others; and build a secure base from which they can venture out to explore their environment while still feeling protected. We as a society must come to an understanding that caregivers are absolutely central to the development of babies into productive citizens. The relationships with the people who care for them, and the conditions under which we allow those relationships to be conducted, play a significant role in the person a baby will grow into and how that person will eventually contribute to society. Given the many hours babies spend with nonparental caregivers, interactions with those caregivers are among the most impactful toward babies' development. At this time, the quality of infant/toddler care in the United States is sorely lacking, and it puts our babies at risk. Listen to the words of a new mother of a 6-month-old who is also a professional consultant to child-care centers:

> What I fear most about bringing my son to child care is what I saw when I consulted with them. You do have the exceptional teachers that really tune into each of the children's individual needs, but you also have teachers who are more disengaged, with kind of a glazed look. I was terrified of having my child in a place where teachers may be overwhelmed or emotionally unavailable. I think it's a little ironic that I work in a field to promote quality of child care, and I feel really ambivalent about sending my own child to child care.

CHAPTER 6

What the Toddler Needs from 15 to 36 Months
The Stage of Self-Definition

He has just begun to be aware that you and he are separate people; he does not yet take it comfortably for granted. Some of the time he asserts this new-found individuality, yelling "No!" and "Let me!," fighting your control and his own need for your help each time an issue presents itself. But some of the time he clings to you, crying when you leave the room, holding up his arms to be carried, demanding with open mouth that you should feed him.

—Penelope Leach, *Understanding Your Toddler*

At about 15 months of age, an infant's brain moves into a new stage of experience-dependent development. Babies, now toddlers, use the skills and brain structures they have been developing and the lessons they have learned from their relationships with caregivers and others to build a conscious sense of self. Intellectually and socially, they are beginning to develop an awareness of their separateness from their caregivers and a sense of themselves as unique individuals (Vaughn, Kopp, & Krakow, 1984). With the help of their caregivers and based on their relationships with others, including peers, they are learning to process information that will prepare them to develop moral and ethical codes, to better control their impulses and emotions, and to learn the rules of the culture, society, and family into which they were born. Along the way, they will form opinions of themselves and their worth, begin to judge the behaviors of others, feel shame and embarrassment with regard to their behaviors and how they perceive themselves, and become very sensitive to the judgments of others. This is major self-defining work that gets it started and sets its foundations before the child is 3 years old.

This stage of life is marked by rapid changes in toddlers' intellectual, language, social, and perceptual/motor development. During this stage, toddlers are able to use their bodies to do all kinds of things. Toward the middle of this stage, they can run fast, climb high, and hurt others when they hit them (Brownell & Kopp, 2007). By age 2, an explosion of spoken language has usually occurred, with children knowing and being able to speak many words, using complex sentence structures, and rapidly expanding the amount of their verbal communications with others (McQuiston & Kloczko, 2011). The growing sophistication of their language use and understanding helps them to engage others in ways that make it easier for them to understand the social environments in which they live. During this stage, children are beginning to understand the roles they are expected to play in their families and communities (California Department of Education, 2006). Well into toddlerhood, they have increased their ability to focus their attention on topics, people, and objects chosen by others, and they wrestle with the challenges of choosing to do so.

THE SOCIAL WOMB, PART 3: A TIME OF IDENTITY BUILDING

With children's newly developed abilities comes an increased understanding that they, as individuals, have choices, and with that understanding comes an awareness that they also have responsibilities. At this stage, their relationships with their caregivers subtly change. Because they are equipped with newfound skills and maturity, they are now expected by their caregivers to begin to comply with adult requests, to delay gratification, to start to control their own behaviors, and to behave in culturally and socially appropriate ways (Fox & Calkins, 2003).

As a child's brain grows to look more and more like an adult brain, it also starts to function more like an adult brain. Around 18 months of age, with the development of the frontal lobes, children are able to call forth a mental image of their caregivers when in distress. Children with secure attachments to their caregivers (as discussed in Chapter 5) can use these images for self-soothing memories, as a way to regulate their emotions. Children with insecure attachments can also access memories of past interactions with caregivers, but these memories are likely to create feelings of anxiety or avoidance rather than be self-soothing. This is why the interactions that have been happening between babies and their caregivers before this point in their development are so important: The way they have been treated and the memories of that treatment are incorporated into their brain circuitry and influence both their current sense of emotional well-being and how they will interact with others in the present and future (Siegel, 1999).

By 24 months of age, toddlers' brains have matured enough that they can remember events from the relatively distant past. They have gained a sense of time and the ability to hold expectations about sequences of events, and they are surprised when things don't play out in the expected sequence. They have also gained the ability to create spatial maps of the location of objects and places in the environments they have explored (Siegel, 1999). As children gain the ability to remember events in their lives, they incorporate information from their past experiences into the present, to use in evaluating current experiences. Their perceptions of what is happening in the present are colored by both the quality and the content of their past experiences; for example, children who are neglected or treated harshly will draw on those memories and have expectations as to what will happen to them next. Children use their memories to help them judge what appropriate action to take in the present, and, without knowing it, they will develop a style of interacting with others based on those memories. The way caregivers interacted with children as babies also impacts the cognitive richness of memories held. Children whose caregivers spoke to them often, shared rich background information about events, and asked open-ended questions about past experiences were found to have more comprehensive and detailed autobiographical memories than children whose caregivers provided them with less detail and asked more closed-ended questions (Laible, 2004).

It is important to remember how much a child's functioning, in all developmental domains, is influenced by the quality of the day-to-day give-and-take between caregiver and child. The pleasure and delight that babies get from interaction drives them to relate to others more frequently and more skillfully. It also drives development of other skills. The less pleasure and delight a child experiences in interaction, the less open the child becomes to interaction. In light of this, one must remember how much toddlers are taking in from seemingly simple interactions with those who care for them. All interactions between a caregiver and a baby send messages, from tone of voice to movement of head, mouth, and eyebrows. Babies are built to perceive and appreciate the holistic messages transmitted and communicated to them and shape their brains accordingly. That is why it is important to think about the knowledge and character of all those who care for babies including nannies and out-of-home caregivers.

The Self-Conscious Emotions

One of the most important developments during this stage of brain growth is the emergence of self-conscious emotions, such as pride, shame, and embarrassment. As children come to understand that they are being perceived by others and judged by others, they start to relate differently to others. During this stage, children become quite sensitive to the judgments of others, particularly as they relate to the child's actions and emotions. For example, at 2 years of age, toddlers may exhibit embarrassment when praised effusively. When an older toddler does something that is funny to an adult and the adult laughs in a way that he or she thinks is good-natured, the toddler might cry or run to a caregiver for protection. This shows that the toddler understands this laughter as a negative evaluation and is hurt by it. During this time of life, babies are also quite sensitive to negative evaluations relating to their inability to control bodily functions and emotional expression, two areas of development that are major challenges to them and that they are struggling to master. Sensitive, supportive interactions around these and other touchy topics help children develop strategies for modulating their emotional responses to accept and control mistakes and learn from them, whereas critical and/or dismissive interactions are likely to increase the stress of these already challenging and emotionally laden situations. How children will act and relate to others, children and adults, in the future is influenced by these interactions with caregivers. This is another instance in which caregivers' actions can have a lasting effect on how children come to see themselves and others.

The Development of Conscience

The first signs of conscience, or morality, appear at this stage of life, and, like much of the child's other development, this occurs in the context of caregiver/child relationships and is influenced by security of attachment (Kochanska, Koenig, Barry, Kim, & Yoon, 2010). Toddlers who are securely attached to their primary caregivers tend to be more receptive to the kinds of parenting strategies that promote conscience development. Conscience develops through what is learned from experiences that toddlers have within their families and other social contexts, such as early education settings. Those who demonstrate greater internalization of parental rules and greater empathy toward their mothers tend to have greater social competence and exhibit more prosocial behaviors in kindergarten, 1st grade, and 2nd grade (Kochanska, Aksan, Knaack, & Rhines, 2004). What toddlers experience and witness in their day-to-day life forms their expectations for what constitutes appropriate behavior toward others (Barry & Kochanska, 2010). Based on the evaluations of others, toddlers come to define behaviors as "good" or "bad"; they come to define themselves as "good" or "bad" in the same way.

The Building of Peer Relationships

As toddlers grow in their abilities to use language, manipulate symbols, and participate in pretend play, they are driven to spend more time interacting with other children (Howes & Matheson, 1992). At around 24 months of age, interactions with peers become crucial for the learning of personal space and boundary rules and for the development of friendships (Brownell, Ramani, & Zerwas, 2006). At this point in their development, children are starting to develop friendships that are characterized by mutual preference, mutual enjoyment, and the ability to engage in skillful interaction together (Howes, 1983). Researchers have found that when toddlers have the opportunity to interact within stable friend dyads, they are more likely to engage in complex interactions (Howes & Matheson, 1992). This suggests that friendships can help facilitate children's social and interactional competence. Children who were observed to participate in peer relationships in child care were found to be more gregarious, engage in more complex play, and display more behavioral flexibility than those who mostly played alone. Those who had secure attachment relationships with their teachers were observed to more easily form peer relationships, and these children displayed fewer withdrawn behaviors and less hostile aggression toward peers (Howes, Hamilton, & Matheson,

1994). Similar results were found in Israeli infants who were securely attached to their infant teachers, and attachment security was also predictive of more empathic behavior toward peers at age 5 (Oppenheim, Sagi, & Lamb, 1988).

The teacher/child relationship also impacts peer relationships (Howes, Hamilton, & Matheson, 1994). Positive teacher mediation (e.g., verbal or physical assistance) contributed to children being accepted by their peers, whereas negative teacher mediation (interruption, punishment, or separation) was related to hostile aggression among peers. These findings illustrate another area—the area of establishing friendships—in which successful toddler functioning is influenced by caregiver/child interaction.

The Development of Effortful Control and Executive Function

The regulation of one's own behavior has often been cited as a prerequisite to success in life (Bierman, Nix, Greenberg, Blair, & Domitrovich, 2008; Blair, 2002; Denham, 2006; Diamond, 2010; Snow, 2006). This behavior regulation, referred to in this section as *effortful control*, is characterized by the ability to voluntarily focus and shift attention and to voluntarily inhibit or initiate behaviors, including behaviors such as delaying; these processes are integral to emotion regulation (Caspi & Shiner, 2006; Kieras, Tobin, Graziano, & Rothbart, 2005; Saarni, Campos, Camras, & Witherington, 2006). Children's ability to understand, maintain, and flexibly use rules, coupled with their ability to voluntarily and selectively attend to things while managing anxiety, anger, and other negative emotions, has been shown to directly relate to school success. Although much of the development of these skills and abilities takes place after age 3, the foundations for the attainment of these skills are based in infancy.

At about 18 months of age, there is rapid development in a baby's prefrontal cortex and its linking with other parts of the brain. Children start to order and organize their thinking and feeling by using, in combination, the executive function skills of the following:

- *Working memory*—the capacity to hold and manipulate information in our heads over short periods of time
- *Inhibitory control*—the skills we use to master and filter our thoughts and impulses so we can resist temptations and distractions, as well as to pause and think before we act
- *Mental flexibility*—the capacity to nimbly switch gears and adjust to changed demands, priorities, or perspectives (National Scientific Council on the Developing Child, 2011)

By using these skills, children are making major advances in the development of skills that will help them work with and get along with others—that is, if they get help from their caregivers (Lagattuta & Wellman, 2002; Laible, 2004; Thompson & Meyer, 2007). At this stage, children should be helped by caregivers to practice some of the skills they will be expected to master in preschool, such as retaining things in their memory, controlling their anxiety after they make a mistake, controlling their temper when they don't get their way, testing and changing hypotheses, and stopping and thinking before they act (Blair, Zelazo, & Greenberg, 2005; Jones, Rothbart, & Posner, 2003). It has also been found that if children are helped to develop these skills early on, they will be more amenable to developing them to higher levels as students when they get to school (Consortium on the School-based Promotion of Social Competence, 1994; Halberstadt, Denham, & Dunsmore, 2001).

One particularly thorny issue, if children don't receive help with it, is self-regulation. If children don't learn this skill early on, troubles can quickly escalate. Researchers have found that children who can't self-regulate their behavior, once in school, have difficulty establishing relationships with teachers and have trouble interacting with peers around learning tasks (Trentacosta & Izard, 2007).

The availability of responsive parents at home and well-trained, responsive caregivers in child care is once again key. Toddlers need to be with adults who understand them—their temperaments, their strengths and weaknesses—and are able to use this knowledge to help them gain self-control. Learning effortful control and developing executive function skills is hard work; a knowledgeable helper is a great gift for a child making the transition from an infant, with few expectations for self-regulation and focused attention, to a preschooler facing expectations of these abilities. During this period of transition, children need caregivers who first provide external regulation to the child and then provide opportunities for the child to practice the new abilities. Activities instigated by a caregiver for 2-year-olds, such as intentional pretend play in which children are given specific roles to play for brief periods of time, can help toddlers gain these skills. Mostly, however, children learn important discipline and thinking skills through day-to-day exchanges with caregivers. They witness and learn from their caregivers as the caregivers model both self-control and mental flexibility. Emotional communications with their caregivers teach them about feelings and thoughts triggered during interactions and how to practice self-control. They benefit from caregivers' guidance relating to their actions when they are interacting with peers. Thus, during this formative period, children are dependent on their caregivers for help with the development of important skill sets needed for success in school and later life, and with the construction of patterns of thinking and feeling that will be set down in their brains. Unfortunately most caregivers are not currently trained to provide this help.

SUPPORTS NECESSARY TO SUSTAIN DEVELOPMENT BETWEEN 15 AND 36 MONTHS

Well-baby care should continue until the 24th month. After 24 months, it can be transitioned into whatever ongoing health services are provided to the family. All of the supports recommended in Chapter 5 to ensure the quality and affordability of child care continue to be necessary at this stage as well.

One new support needed is special training for all infant/toddler caregivers in two content areas: training in the crucial role caregivers play in the development of a child's first sense of self, and how caregivers can best facilitate that development; and training in ways to facilitate children's development of effortful control and executive function skills (Child Trends, 2010; Leong, 2011).

Successfully implementing this training may be difficult in practice, as the relatively sophisticated concepts it involves may be challenging to learn without a strong background in early childhood education. Unfortunately, state educational requirements for child-care providers are currently quite low. The National Association of Child Care Resource and Referral Agencies (2011b) reported that, as of 2011:

- Sixteen states (Alabama, Arizona, Indiana, Kansas, Kentucky, Maine, Michigan, New Hampshire, North Carolina, North Dakota, Ohio, South Carolina, Tennessee, Texas, Washington, and West Virginia) require a lead teacher in a child-care classroom to have a high school diploma or GED.
- Sixteen states (Alaska, Arkansas, Georgia, Idaho, Iowa, Louisiana, Mississippi, Missouri, Montana, Nebraska, Nevada, New Mexico, Oregon, South Dakota, Utah, and Wyoming) do not require a lead teacher in a child-care classroom to have a high school diploma or GED.
- The remaining 18 states do not require any specific number of training hours before working in a child-care center.

One study of the child-care workforce revealed that almost half of providers in regulated child-care settings (including 20% of child-care center teachers, 43% of center assistants, and 44% of family child-care providers) enter the profession with a high school education or less (Zigler, Marsland, & Lord, 2009).

In the following interview excerpts, two program directors interviewed for this book discuss their concerns about the quality of infant/toddler care and what that means for children:

> I have a center director who recently shared with me that she can't afford high-quality, well-trained infant/toddler teachers. [She] can't afford to attract them and to retain them, and because of that, [she knows] what type of quality is being provided in their setting with a teacher that is less skilled and less educated in the art and science of caring for infants and toddlers, and how disappointing that is, and how scared she is about being able to improve the program quality when the level is so low.

> It's really a bit of an ethical dilemma for us. We know what the minimum standards of quality care are, and sometimes we're caught in a situation where we have to make a choice of either cutting corners and providing what we know to be substandard care or cutting costs altogether and not being able to offer care for infants and toddlers at all.

CHAPTER 7

Recommended Supports and Services for Babies and Their Families

Each of us must come to care about everyone else's children. We must recognize that the welfare of our children is intimately linked to the welfare of all other people's children. After all, when one of our children needs life-saving surgery, someone else's child will perform it. If one of our children is harmed by violence, someone else's child will be responsible for the violent act. The good life for our own children can be secured only if a good life is secured for all other people's children.

—Lilian Katz

Building on the discussions in the other chapters in Part II, this chapter presents 20 recommendations for the direct and indirect supports that families need to help with the care of their babies. It is written with the healthy, unimpeded development of babies in mind. The United States is one of the most forward-looking, powerful nations in the world; thus, we should have policies and practices in place that prioritize the care and protection of babies. The following recommendations are organized according to the topics in Chapters 3–6 and include references to appendices that provide further, more detailed information.

PRECONCEPTION

Today, the greatest opportunities for further improvement in pregnancy outcomes—in improving the health of women and their children—lie in prevention strategies that must be implemented prior to conception to be effective. . . .
The time has come to move forward to the next maternal and child health frontier of "prevention" by acting on the recommendations of professional organizations and implementing scientifically proven interventions to further improve pregnancy outcomes.

—Hani K. Atrash et al., *Preconception Care for Improving Perinatal Outcomes*

Recommendation 1: A multimedia public education campaign should be conducted to provide all women of childbearing age with information on how their preconception health and behaviors can influence the development of a fetus.

- To be effective, the campaign should use communication tools that reach women in varying age, literacy, health literacy, cultural, and linguistic demographics.
- This public health and education campaign should include a component directed to health professionals.
- To decrease dissemination costs, the campaign may be incorporated into other campaigns directed at these populations.

Recommendation 2: All obstetricians, gynecologists, general practitioners, and public health nurses serving women of childbearing age should receive in-service training on taking future fetal development into account during yearly check-ups and when screening, assessment, and counseling are conducted.

- Such trainings should earn participants continuing-education credits.
- Professional credentialing organizations should make such training obligatory in order for participants to receive a credential.
- Such training should constitute an appropriate billable health cost.

Recommendation 3: Preconception counseling and services should be included in health-care coverage for all women of childbearing age, regardless of their socioeconomic status.

Recommendation 4: As part of health-insurance coverage, intervention services should be provided for women with identified risks.

- Initial focus should be on high-priority interventions.
- The proportion of women who receive follow-up interventions related to preconception screenings should be increased by 50%.

PREGNANCY

Almost 4 million American women give birth every year and nearly one third of them will have some kind of pregnancy-related complication. Those who don't get adequate prenatal care run the risk that such complications will go undetected or won't be dealt with soon enough. That, in turn, can lead to potentially serious consequences for both the mother and her baby.

—National Development and Research Institutes

Recommendation 5: Free or affordable health care should be provided to pregnant women during their pregnancy. The Centers for Disease Control and Prevention have established the following recommendations for the provision of high-quality pregnancy care:

- regular check-ups
- counseling
- evaluation
- prevention

- risk assessment
- screening and early interventions

Appendix C contains a chart of more specific health-care recommendations from the U.S. Department of Health and Human Services (2011c).

Recommendation 6: Paid leave and job protection should be provided for pregnant women during the last month of pregnancy, to ensure the health and safety of both the mother and the fetus.

Recommendation 7: A national information campaign addressing issues that support a healthy pregnancy should be conducted.

- This campaign may be integrated with the preconception campaign.
- The campaign should target the general public, not just pregnant women.

THE FIRST 9 MONTHS

Policy initiatives that promote supportive relationships and rich learning opportunities for young children create a strong foundation for high school achievement followed by greater productivity in the workplace and solid citizenship in the community.

—National Scientific Council on the Developing Child

Recommendation 8: All families' access to affordable health coverage for babies should be guaranteed, regardless of family income.

- Coverage should include necessary inoculations, developmental screening to identify physical and behavioral needs, and intervention services (if required).
- A provision currently exists to include coverage for these recommended services under the Patient Protection and Affordable Care Act (PPAC), scheduled to be implemented in 2014.

Recommendation 9: Provide affordable or free intervention services for children with identified special needs and for families in crisis.

Recommendation 10: Paid parental leave, shareable between parents, should be provided for the first 9 months after a baby's birth. Given the impact of bonding on the baby's brain development during this time period, the following terms should apply:

- Full compensation should be provided for 6 months of leave or 80% compensation for 9 months of leave.
- Financing of the program should be a combination of employer/ employee contributions, similar to disability tax, and a specific federal tax for this purpose.
- Variable leave time should be made available to primary and secondary parenting figures, with the primary caregiver granted the entire time period and the secondary caregiver eligible for 1 month of leave time.
- Eligibility for leave should depend on the parent having accumulated 1,000 work hours for the employer during the previous year, or at least an average of 1 day a week for 3 or more continuous years.
- Leave-program participation should not be limited according to the size of a participating business.

See Appendix D for a sampling of national paid-leave policies in other countries.

Recommendation 11: For the first 2 years of life, affordable, in-home well-baby care should be provided.

- The following should be included:
  - » Guidance by trained professionals in parenting and healthy development
  - » Counseling on early emotional, social, language, intellectual, and perceptual/motor development
- The screenings and other services referred to in Recommendation 8 could be performed as part of these visits.
- The numbers of visits and types of services should vary based on case-specific circumstances, but the typical well-baby care visit schedule for the first 9 months is as follows:

> » 5 to 7 days from hospital discharge
> » 2 weeks
> » 1 month
> » 2 months
> » 3 months
> » 4 months
> » 6 months
> » 9 months

See Appendix E for information about well-baby care services in other countries.

FROM 7 TO 18 MONTHS

The essence of quality in early childhood services is embodied in the expertise and skills of the staff and their capacity to build positive relationships with young children. The striking shortage of well-trained personnel in the field today indicates that substantial investments in training, recruiting, compensating, and retaining a high-quality workforce must be a top priority.

—National Scientific Council on the Developing Child

Recommendation 12: Assistance in transitioning babies into child care should be provided to parents.

- Crucial topics to be addressed include the following:
  - » Identifying and ensuring quality care
  - » Regular communications with caregivers
  - » How to handle drop-offs during the first month
- If well-baby care visits are in place, integrate this information as part of those visits.
- This recommendation should apply even if children move into child care before 7 months.

Recommendation 13: Affordable, high-quality infant/toddler care should be made accessible to all. Federal, state, and/or workplace subsidies should be awarded to care providers to ensure that high-quality care is affordable.

Recommendation 14: Infant/toddler care regulations that ensure safe, engaging, and intimate settings should be enforced. See Appendix B for Program for Infant/Toddler Care (PITC) guidelines for quality infant/toddler care.

Recommendation 15: Steps should be taken to ensure that infant/toddler care providers receive compensation and health benefits on par with those of K–12 schoolteachers.

Recommendation 16: Certification, credentialing, and training should be required for all infant/toddler care providers. See Appendix F for National Association of Child Care Resource and Referral Agencies (NACCRRA) recommendations for certification and credentialing and Program for Infant/Toddler Care (PITC) recommendations for the training for infant/toddler care providers.

Recommendation 17: Infant/toddler care providers should be provided with access to consulting professionals in the areas of early childhood mental health, special education, and child development to help with early identification of and interventions for developmental issues.

FROM 15 TO 36 MONTHS

National research underscores that quality child care is contingent upon the special training that caregivers receive in the profession of early childhood development. Both formal education levels and recent, specialized training in child development have been found quite consistently to be associated with high-quality interactions and children's development. Teachers with a Child Development Associate (CDA) provide higher quality early learning experiences than those with only a high school diploma. And teachers with college degrees provide superior early learning experiences.

—ZERO TO THREE

Recommendation 18: Well-baby care should continue as in the previous age group, until the 24th month. At that point, care should be transitioned into the family's ongoing health services.

Recommendation 19: All of the recommendations pertaining to child care regulations and infant/toddler caregivers for the previous age group continue to be necessary for this age group.

Recommendation 20: Special training beyond that recommended in Recommendation 16 should be provided for all infant/toddler caregivers serving children from 15 to 36 months of age.

- Caregivers should be trained to understand their crucial role in a child's development of sense of self and how they can best facilitate that development.
- Caregivers should be trained on how to facilitate the development of intentional control and executive function skills.

For information on the importance of these training topics, see the sources listed in Appendix G from Harvard University's Center on the Developing Child.

SUPPORTING BABIES' HEALTHY DEVELOPMENT

I understand that acting on these recommendations would require significant new services compared to what already exists in this country, but the difference between the proposed services and services already being provided in other countries is less dramatic. These services are needed and necessary. Without them, babies' developmental trajectories are put in jeopardy.

··

PART III

Why It Makes Sense to Help Families Meet the Needs of their Babies

CHAPTER 8

Economic Benefits of Investment in U.S. Babies

We live in an age of human capital being the most important capital that any country has, and the only way America can out-compete the rest of the world is if we out-educate the rest of the world . . . The only way we can do that is making sure every child gets a healthy start and a rich early learning experience.

—Kathleen Sebelius,
U.S. Secretary of Health and Human Services

I write this chapter with great reluctance because I do not believe that protecting our children should require much of an economic justification. Over the last 47 years, my professional experiences have placed me with too many babies who have been negatively affected by inadequate conditions—starting in the womb and continuing through low-quality child care. I've seen too many damaged babies, preschoolers, and elementary school students to believe we need any justification for protecting children other than keeping them from harm.

I'm not an economist. I haven't done extensive research on the financial benefits of treating babies, though a number of economists have in the last 20 years, and I've cited some of their work in this chapter and included recommended readings in Appendix H. However, I have seen, firsthand, the benefits that quality home-visitation programs, high-quality infant/toddler care, and professional consultation can have for young children.

I understand that providing the services I've recommended in this book will be quite expensive. Luckily, in many instances, implementing them will save money in both the short run and the long run. Nonetheless, I want to state, at the outset, that the economics set forth in this chapter shouldn't be the reason our country invests in the very young. Instead, I hope that common decency and common sense will drive our decision-making. In my opinion, the most important statistic presented in this chapter—more telling than any particular cost saving associated with any specific service—is that the cost of all of the recommendations presented in Chapter 7 would be less than 1% of the U.S. gross domestic product (GDP)—in fact, probably less than half a percent. This tells me that caring for babies in the United States is more about prioritizing spending than it is about finding revenue. With this caveat in mind, this chapter discusses how supporting babies' developmental needs can result in cost savings that families, businesses, and governments may benefit from. While it does not provide a complete list of potential cost savings, I believe that the information in this chapter is sufficient to make a financial argument for better services for U.S. babies.

PRECONCEPTION HEALTH SERVICES

In 2006, the Centers for Disease Control and Prevention reported that quality preconception health services reduce infant mortality, pregnancy complications, birth defects, and long-term developmental problems, and help accelerate postpartum recovery (Centers for Disease Control and Prevention, 2006). A 2006 analysis of comprehensive preconception care provided support for the money-saving aspect of improved outcomes in these areas (Grosse, Sotnikkov, Leatherman, & Curtis, 2006). This study found that every dollar spent on preconception care saved $1.60 on maternal and fetal care costs. Other studies have shown further savings as preconception care reduces the rate of neonatal intensive care unit (NICU) hospitalizations among infants; according to Grosse et al. (2006), a single dollar of preconception investment can save as much as $5.19. These savings are significant enough to draw the attention of the business world. Based on a recent assessment of pregnant women and nonpregnant women of childbearing age, the National Business Group on Health (2007, p. 2) identified four clear benefits that improved preconception health services would provide for both business and government employers:

- *Lowered health-care costs.* Healthy women and children use fewer costly health-care services (such as hospitalization) and thus have lower total health-care costs.
- *Increased productivity.* When children are born and develop healthily, women are less likely to need family medical leave, personal sick leave, or paid time off to care for their health needs.
- *Improved retention/reduced turnover.* Women who have healthy, complication-free pregnancies are able to work longer during their pregnancies and return to work sooner after delivery as compared to women who suffer complications. Similarly, parents with healthy children are less likely to leave the workforce or cut back their work hours compared to the parents of children with chronic illnesses or severe disabilities.
- *A healthier future workforce.* Today's children and adolescents are tomorrow's workforce.

In the United States, the newness of addressing issues of fetal-development concerns with women who are not yet pregnant means that many women, from all socioeconomic backgrounds, are not yet receiving these services. This represents an opportunity for substantial improvements in outcomes for a relatively small investment—the cost of information sharing, counseling, assessment, and (when necessary) intervention.

PREGNANCY SERVICES

In their study previously discussed, the National Business Group on Health (2007) concluded, "A pregnancy beset by complications is more costly to employers than a healthy pregnancy; and sick mothers and newborns are more costly to employers than healthy ones. Facilitating healthy pregnancies is in the best interest of both employers and employees" (p. 11). Regarding actual cost savings from prenatal-care services, the National Committee for Quality Assurance found that "for every dollar spent on prenatal care, employers can expect a savings of $3.33 for postnatal care and $4.63 in long-term morbidity costs" (National Business Group on Health, 2007, p. 3).

While this finding is fairly straightforward, related findings can be hard to parse. For example, the nation spends approximately $3.2 billion annually to treat asthma in children and adolescents (Harvard Medical School, 2004). This disease often starts in the womb and can be influenced by a mother's preconception health, with research showing that women who smoke while pregnant are more likely to deliver infants with asthma and/or other respiratory problems (National Business Group on Health, 2007).

Based on the link between preconception counseling and reduction in smoking during pregnancy, it can be assumed that the $3.2 billion figure would have been even higher without the preconception health services that currently exist. In support of this conclusion, the U.S. Public Health Service (2000) has stated that tobacco-cessation treatment for pregnant women is one of the most cost-saving preventive services provided in this country. Several clinical trials have drawn even more direct evidentiary links between smoking cessation and health-care cost savings. A study conducted by Marks, Koplan, Hogue, and Dalmat (1990) found that every dollar spent on smoking-cessation programs results in $6 of future health-care savings.

Smoking-cessation counseling is only one of many services provided during prenatal visits; a single prenatal visit will often screen and tackle many topics, which means that the cost savings resulting from smoking cessation are only part of the savings based on a visit. For example, these visits commonly identify and address issues of alcohol misuse, for which a single dollar of prevention spending can save $4 in the long term (Fleming et al., 2002; Gentilello, Ebel, Wickizer, Salkever, & Rivara, 2005).

The future cost savings of visits are also influenced by the quality of the visit, not only the specific topics discussed. As discussed in earlier chapters, effective prenatal services adapt treatment and numbers of visits on a case-by-case basis, based on early assessments; conducting assessments early allows health-care providers to identify and respond to high-priority risks. Research has shown that quickly identifying and handling high-risk conditions generates savings, usually as a result of reducing hospital and NICU admission rates among newborns. Depending on the population, the savings generated through effective prenatal care range from $1,768 to $5,560 per infant/mother pair (Reece, Leguizamon, Silva, Whiteman, & Smith, 2002; Ross, Sandhu,

Bemis, Nessim, Bragonier, & Hobel, 1994). Based on these studies as well as many others, it can be concluded that prenatal care services reduce both short-term health-care costs and long-term costs of compensatory services.

WELL-BABY CARE SERVICES

Once a child is born, receiving in-home well-baby care visits reduces the child's overall health-care costs. Well-baby care visits often focus on breastfeeding, encouraging mothers to breastfeed and providing assistance and guidance when required. This focus results in higher numbers of mothers who start or continue breastfeeding, in comparison to mothers who do not receive in-home care visits (Kitzman et al., 2000; Task Force on Community Preventive Services, 2003). Breastfeeding has been linked to reduced rates of ear, gastrointestinal, and urinary tract infections; diabetes; childhood leukemia; and Sudden Infant Death Syndrome (Chung et al., 2008; Dyson, McCormick, & Renfrew, 2005).

Compared to breastfed infants, formula-fed infants cost the health-care system more money because of their increased rates of illness and hospitalization. In just their first year of life, never-breastfed infants (compared to breastfed infants) experience 2,033 additional office visits, 212 additional days of hospitalization, and 609 more prescriptions per 1,000 infants. This additional health care carries costs of between $331 and $475 per infant (Ball & Wright, 1999; Kramer & Kakuma, 2002; Oddy et al., 2003). Additionally, mothers who do not breastfeed have an increased risk of developing breast or ovarian cancer (Ip et al., 2007; Stuebe, 2009). According to Bartick and Reinhold (2010), services that promote breastfeeding exclusively for at least the first 6 months of life could save the United States $13 billion in health-care costs and other costs each year.

Well-baby care visits have also been shown to decrease child abuse and neglect, as well as family tobacco and alcohol use; reduce risks of subsequent pregnancies; and increase parents' workforce participation and family income, leading to even more cost savings (Kitzman et al., 2000; Minnesota Center for Health Statistics, 2010; Minnesota Department of Health, 2009; Task Force on Community Preventive Services, 2003). A study of the Elmira Prenatal/Early Infancy Project, which provided weekly home visits from a nurse practitioner, found that, for high-risk groups of children enrolled in the project, every $1 invested produced a $6.92 return (Olds, Henderson, Phelps, Kitzman, & Hanks, 1993).

In well-baby care, as with other services, quality matters. Hakim and Ronsaville (2002) found that well-baby care service has to be consistent and thorough to really be effective. They found that incomplete well-baby care in the first 6 months significantly increased the likelihood that babies would visit an emergency department for an upper respiratory tract infection, gastroenteritis, or asthma. Further, babies with incomplete care were 60% more likely to visit a hospital emergency room for any cause, compared to babies who were up-to-date on their well-baby care, increasing the cost of their overall care.

Just as with preconception and prenatal care, it's clear that quality well-baby care services can result in major savings.

GUARANTEED HEALTH-CARE COVERAGE
FOR FAMILIES WITH CHILDREN UNDER AGE 3

Many of the potential savings that would come from guaranteed health-care coverage for families are related to the waste, inefficiency, and unnecessary services of our current health-care services. However, as components of the Patient Protection and Affordable Care Act (PPACA) go into effect, beginning in 2014, the delivery of health-care services in the United States will change dramatically. These changes are designed, in part, to make our health-care system more cost efficient, and the projected savings from these changes are directly relevant to the services recommended in this book. Although the PPACA does not provide universal coverage, it is a step toward universal coverage, and it is constructed to yield cost benefits in 20 years if we modify our health-care delivery system for greater effectiveness (Cutler, 2010; National Institutes of Health, 2010). But modification is necessary. Dr. David Cutler (2010) states; "Estimates suggest that anywhere from 30 to 50% of medical spending is not needed to realize the outcomes we achieve—a waste of about $1 trillion annually" (p. 1133).

Universal Provision of Inoculations for Young Children

Study after study shows that societies benefit when all children receive recommended immunizations, and, in the United States, we can take pride in the success of our nearly universal provision of inoculations for children. Vaccines have been proven to be cost effective, and numerous studies show that the cost of providing common vaccines to children and adolescents is far less expensive than that of treating diseases that are preventable by vaccines. Cost-benefit analyses indicate that vaccination against most common childhood diseases results in large returns on investment: for every dollar spent on vaccination, between $10 and $18 are saved in medical and indirect costs (Adetunji, Macklin, Patel, & Kinsinger, 2003; Every Child by Two, 2012; National Business Group on Health, 2007). One study showed that, while the cost of providing the Seven-Vaccine Routine Childhood Immunization series to children was estimated at $2.3 billion (direct) and $2.8 billion (societal), the cost of treating the diseases prevented by the immunization series would amount to $12.3 billion in direct costs and $46.6 billion in societal costs (Zhou et al., 2005). With benefits so clearly greater than costs, inoculation is a good test case for the value of providing universal health services.

Universal Provision of Screening for Young Children

Although periodic screening for young children is not as widely available as inoculation, the cost-benefit analyses quite clearly show that the screenings pay for themselves. The World Health Organization recently found an economic benefit of $17 saved for every $1 invested in programs that screen, identify, and treat children at risk of developmental delay. Their report concludes that the earlier the intervention, the lower the overall cost (Irwin, Siddiqi, & Hertzman, 2007). The Centers for Disease Control and Prevention report similar findings specifically for babies, stating that the newborn screenings presently available can save between $500,000 and $1 million in lifetime costs per disability prevented (Grosse, 2004). This finding led the authors of the Florida Department of Health's 2010 document *Prevention Pays* to conclude, "The lifetime savings for these conditions in Florida far exceed the costs of implementing and maintaining a statewide newborn screening program" (Office of Health Statistics and Assessment, 2010, p. 10).

The possibility that delivery reforms will improve cost effectiveness, the current evidence that nearly universal provision of inoculations is a savings boon, and the long-term payoffs of universal early screening—all point toward an argument for providing universal health care for families with babies.

PAID LEAVE AND QUALITY INFANT/TODDLER CARE

Of all of the services recommended in this book, paid leave and quality infant/toddler care carry the heftiest up-front price tags. Since the United States does not have a national paid-leave policy, no national data on potential savings are available. There is, however, information derived from state initiatives in California and New Jersey. In a recent study of California's paid-leave program,

Appelbaum and Milkman (2011) found that the program had minimal impact on businesses' bottom lines while benefiting families. Structured similarly to unemployment insurance, the program had no direct cost to employers, and it was found to increase the likelihood that workers in low-quality jobs would return to work after paid leave. On average, mothers who took advantage of the program doubled the number of weeks they breastfed their children, and the program also saw a substantial increase in men taking time to bond with a new child (from 17% to 26%).

While an overall lack of high-quality infant/toddler care means there's little direct evidence of the savings it can provide, a great deal of data point to the cost-effectiveness of early childhood education in general. There are also new ways of analyzing the impact of programs, which show more and more evidence that the long-term economic payoffs of early child services outweigh the initial expense of providing these services.

Early Intervention

As explained in Chapter 2, the link between early experience and brain development has become clearer and clearer in the last 20 years (National Scientific Council on the Developing Child, 2007b). Each year, we discover more about the importance of baby and caretaker interactions for children's brain development and development in general (National Scientific Council on the Developing Child, 2010). We've learned that the timing of certain experiences is extremely important because of sensitive development periods that all children and adults go through. Without certain experiences during these periods, development suffers. The development that occurs during each sensitive period influences the successful negotiation of subsequent periods (National Scientific Council on the Developing Child, 2007b). These findings from neuroscience not only help us better understand development processes but also provide a foundation for cost-benefit analysis.

James Heckman, a Nobel Prize–winning economist from the University of Chicago, has taken the concept of sensitive periods from the neuroscience community and used it as the base for much of his research on the cost benefits of early intervention. Heckman points out how sensitive periods interact with two other traits of development—self-productivity and dynamic complementarity—to explain why early investments in intervention are so effective (Heckman, 2006a). He defines *sensitive periods* as periods of development that are more effective in producing certain capacities and that uniquely facilitate the acquisition of those capacities; these periods augment capacities attained at later stages, because capacities gained at one stage are self-reinforcing and cross-fertilizing at later stages (i.e., *self-productive*), and capacities produced at one stage raise the productivity of investments at subsequent stages (i.e., *dynamic complementarity*) because the foundation upon which subsequent investments are made is more able to efficiently benefit from those investments (Heckman, 2006a). In layperson's terms, the earlier an investment is made, the greater the benefits that will be gained. If investments continue to be made as development proceeds, each will build on and draw from those prior, allowing investments to be utilized more fully and effectively. This concept is why the cost savings identified in this section—both for paid leave and for high-quality infant/toddler care—cite the long-term outcomes that are greatly dependent on the very earliest of experiences.

High-Quality Early Care

Before discussing the evidence of cost savings in these areas, a clarification about the important link between quality services and cost savings is necessary. In Chapter 7, multiple expensive services were recommended as necessary components of providing high-quality infant/toddler child care; these services include training, certification, credentialing, adequate staff compensation and benefits, and the implementation of quality program policies and practices. It's true that if these recommendations are put into place, they will drive up the costs of providing infant/toddler care, compared with current practice. It must be noted, however, that all of the programs that were studied for the cost-benefit analyses reported in this chapter and that were found to have long-term payoffs contained all of the aforementioned components of high-quality care. These programs, though expensive to operate, were found to be of excellent quality. It is likely that services that operate without the aforementioned components won't produce cost-effective outcomes and may damage the chances of infants and toddlers gaining any benefits from care. The point is that, although ensuring high quality of care services is expensive, it is necessary to produce gains in human capacity as well as cost savings.

Independent research by the Frank Porter Graham Child Development Institute at the University of North Carolina–Chapel Hill found that children who started Educare, a high-quality early childhood education program for children from low income families at multiple sites across the country, between birth and age 2 exceeded national averages on measures of school readiness. Additionally, those gains persisted even when controlling for risk factors such as maternal education, race, and parents' ages (Yazejian & Bryant, 2010).

Multiple findings support the position that even high costs can be repaid in the long-term savings. Based on a study of the long-term outcomes of investment in early childhood, Heckman and Masterov (2004) concluded that early monetary investments in human capital yield the highest returns and that the earlier the investment, the higher the return. Researchers from the Center on the Developing Child at Harvard University have supported these conclusions. Based on neuroscience research, they propose that investments in infancy influence how brains are structured and therefore influence future brain functioning and, ultimately, success in life (National Scientific Council on the Developing Child, 2007a).

Figure 8.1 represents one estimation of rates of return on investment in human capital, relative to age. Heckman and colleagues have found that every dollar invested in early childhood programs can lead to between $4 and $17 dollars in savings in later compensatory services, crime reduction, increased schooling, workforce productivity, and reductions in both teenage pregnancy and welfare dependency (Cunha & Heckman, 2007; Heckman, 2006b; Heckman, 2000).

Figure 8.1. Estimated Return on Investment at Different Ages

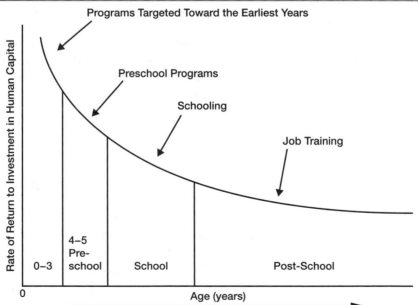

Source: Heckman, 2012

Long-Term Data

After analyzing longitudinal research on early childhood education participants, Lynch (2004) concluded that public investment in comprehensive
early childhood programs for all children from low-income families in the
United States would start paying for itself in 17 years and would generate bil-
lions more than it costs within 25 years. He also estimated a net benefit-to-
cost ratio of 8 to 1 for quality early childhood education services when 71%
of the children served were from middle-income families (compared to 12
to 1 for a program targeted only at children from low-income families). He
predicted that implementing a universal early childhood education program
would eventually give the government a 2 to 1 return on investment and that
within 17 years the annual fiscal benefits to the federal government would
begin exceeding the program's annual costs. The importance of Lynch's work
is that it shows the economic benefits of early investments in all children, not
just those from low-income families.

Other research has supported Lynch's conclusions. In a study conducted
by the Minneapolis Federal Reserve Bank, using evaluation data from the Per-
ry Preschool Program, Rolnick and Grunewald (2003) found a 16% rate of
return on investment in early childhood education, which far exceeded rates
of return for other public-works projects and subsidies to business.

By following up on participants in the Abecedarian Project, a controlled
study of early childhood education that ran from 1972 to 1977, researchers
were able to provide important long-term data about the benefits of providing
disadvantaged children with high-quality educational child care and preschool
between birth and 5 years of age (Frank Porter Graham Child Development
Institute, 2012). The average annual cost of the intervention, in 2012 dollars,
was about $16,000 per child (Bartik, 2011). The follow-up program evalua-
tions gathered data on past program participants at ages 21 and 30. These participants had received one of four interventions:

- child-care/preschool treatment (age 0–5);
- child-care/preschool treatment (age 0–5) and school-age treatment
  (grades 1–3);
- school-age treatment (grades 1–3); or
- no treatment.

When the scores of these groups were compared, researchers found
that, at age 21, educational and life outcomes for the children receiving the

child-care/preschool treatment were far superior to those for the children not receiving the child-care/preschool treatment, including the children receiving only the school-age treatment. They found higher attainment for the child-care/preschool group, compared to the other groups, in reading, mathematics, and years of education completed; much higher percentages of participants who were enrolled in school at age 21, had attended or were attending a 4-year college, and were engaged in skilled jobs; and a much lower percentage who had become teenage parents. It was also found that school-age treatment for a very disadvantaged population only produced marginal impacts (Campbell, Pungello, Miller-Johnson, Burchinal, & Ramey, 2001; Campbell, Ramey, Pungello, Sparling, & Miller-Johnson, 2002; Masse & Barnett, 2002). These findings are fascinating because they reinforce Heckman's conclusions about the importance of timing in the effectiveness of interventions and the influence of the combination of sensitive periods, self-productivity, and dynamic complementarity.

Bartik's (2011) follow-up data on 30-year-old program participants also support Heckman's conclusions. At age 30, compared to age 21, the program participants showed continuing benefit from the intervention, and educational attainment scores continued to grow at an accelerated rate. Between ages 21 and 30, the average years of schooling completed by the program participants rose by 1.1 years, and the percentage of participants with bachelor's degrees increased from 6% to 23%. This can be seen as a significant jump, as Bartik had estimated only a 12% increase based on the results of the age-21 data. Additionally, program participants' increasing rates of full-time employment have been estimated to be statistically significant. From age 21 to age 30, the program participants' average annual income increased by over $12,000, from slightly under $21,000 to slightly over $33,000. These earning estimates show an increase in economic development benefits, per dollar spent, from $2.25 to $2.53, or an increase of over 10% in the benefit-cost ratio (Bartik, 2011).

Another well-studied early intervention is the Child-Parent Center Education Program in Chicago, for which findings for participants up to age 28 are now available (Reynolds, Temple, Ou, Arteaga, & White, 2011). As with the Abecedarian Project, increasingly positive results were found as program participants grew older. This program began with a preschool experience and provided services for up to 6 years after program entry. Similar to the Abecedarian research, when this program's participants were compared with a control group, researchers found higher educational attainment, income, and socioeconomic status, as well as higher rates of health insurance coverage and lower rates of justice-system involvement and substance abuse. Among specific findings of this study, comparing the preschool participants with a control group, are the following:

- 9% more completed high school
- 20% more achieved a moderate or higher level of socioeconomic status
- 19% more carried some level of health insurance coverage
- 28% fewer abused drugs and alcohol
- 22% fewer had a felony arrest
- 45% fewer whose parents were high school dropouts had felony arrests than control-group participants whose parents were high school dropouts

The most positive outcomes found were for those who began services in preschool—especially among males and among children of high school dropouts (Reynolds et al., 2011). Again, these findings support Heckman's conclusions about the power of early intervention.

In a different type of study, Bartik (2006) demonstrated another kind of cost benefit from early childhood investments: using sports stadiums and retail facilities as points of comparison, Bartik showed that investments in early childhood education tend to boost local economic growth and employment without reducing them in other areas, as sports stadiums and retail facilities often do.

The National Scientific Council on the Developing Child (2008) has also described evidence of cost benefits from early care. Seeing that Heckman's and Rolnick and Grunewald's research indicated that school dropout occurred in higher rates among children who were not provided with early childhood services, the Council studied the cost of dropping out of school. It found that, on average, high school dropouts lose a quarter of a million dollars in lifetime earnings and ultimately cost taxpayers up to $288,000 in health care, public safety, and other social program costs.

Comparison Costs

One potential indicator of anticipated overall costs for the services recommended in this book is actual costs in other countries. Gornick and Meyers (2003) reviewed actual costs for family support and early child services in various nations in Europe. They found that, as of 1998, costs in the most generous Nordic countries ranged from 0.5% to 0.7% of gross domestic product (GDP), and expenses in other European countries varied from as little as 0.07% of

GDP to between 0.3% and 0.4% (in France and Germany). By 2002, despite increases in the generosity of the programs, these figures had changed only slightly, with costs ranging between 0.5% and 0.8% of GDP in most generous Nordic countries and from 0.1% to 0.2% of GDP in seven other Western European nations (Austria, Germany, Ireland, the Netherlands, Portugal, Switzerland, and the United Kingdom) (Datta Gupta, Smith, & Verner, 2008).

Based on these data, it seems likely that, if the services that are provided in Western Europe are provided in the United States, as recommended in this book, their cost as a percentage of GDP would be lower in the United States than in the Nordic countries—no higher than 0.4%. Even if this estimate were incorrect, and the cost as a percentage of GDP were more in line with that in the Nordic countries, given the long-term savings found by Heckman and others, the investment would be well worth the initial outlay. An investment of less than 1% of GDP is not a huge risk with the potential benefits so great.

CHAPTER 9

A Final Message

What we need to do now is to rally ourselves and our friends and everyone we possibly can find, around the notion that children really are the future of American society, that if we are a healthy and prosperous society 25 years from now, it's going to be because we had the will to make the investments now that allowed children to meet their full potential. I think that's the challenge before us. It's a challenge that we can meet. . . . We have the knowledge we need to support families and to support children in optimal development.

—Moncrieff Cochran

In writing this book, I hope to make visible how we in the United States are ignoring our babies and the damage this lack of attention to babies can cause to babies, to families, and to our society.

As I have shown, our nation's neglect of babies starts even before they are conceived, continues during pregnancy, is blatantly obvious during babies earliest months of life as evidenced by the absence of paid leave and well-baby care and is capped off by the low quality of infant and toddler care available to families throughout the country. Together, these omissions are the ingredients in a recipe for societal disaster.

It is personally disconcerting to me to witness how policymakers in the United States can ignore the knowledge uncovered over the last 20 years that proves the link between positive early experience and environments and successful functioning in later life. The information we have uncovered about the dependence of robust brain functioning in childhood and adulthood on foundations built in the womb and early infancy alone should signal the need for dramatic shifts in resource allotment. It makes no sense to withhold support of development during critical and sensitive periods of infancy when that policy has been shown to lead to expensive compensatory fixes, school failure, and low-functioning and unhealthy adults.

Yes, it may be expensive to provide needed supports during the first years of life, but we've learned that it's equally expensive not to do so, and that it's a tragic waste of human capital. Ironically, it is quite possible that investment in the early years, as leading economists tell us, can actually save money.

I have been watching Europe closely during the recent economic downswing. The leaders of the European Union hold firm against cutting resources that serve families during children's very early years of development. They argue that, without this early spending, their countries would need to spend much more in compensatory services and that their citizens would not be well enough equipped—physically, intellectually, and emotionally—to handle the 21st-century challenges that lie ahead. They accept that an investment in babies is really an investment in human capital.

We in the United States would do well to consider that line of reasoning. Rather than seeing investments in babies as being a huge drain on resources, we should instead see them as wise investments in the development of human capital. Science is telling us that, if we treat them right, babies can provide wonderful gifts to the society into which they are born. If families and other caregivers are supported by society in providing infants with caring connections, enriching experiences, and healthy and interesting environments, those babies' brains will have a better chance of being structured to start the children off on a path laid with increased chances for personal and communal success.

If we in the United States continue to neglect our babies as we currently do, how will they be equipped to face life? How will we develop citizens who are intellectually competent enough, emotionally secure enough, and physically healthy enough to master the challenges of the rest of this century? What kinds of citizens will we develop?

We must treat our babies better. I hope this book has shown that it is the logical and sensible thing to do.

Risk Factors Needing to Be Addressed During Preconception and Pregnancy

Absence of daily use of vitamin supplements containing folic acid:
Folic acid has been shown to reduce the occurrence of neural tube defects by as much as two-thirds; however, in 2004, 44.8% of preconception women and 19.9% of pregnant women reported not taking vitamins with folic acid (Anderson, Ebrahim, Floyd, & Atrash, 2006).

Anxiety and depression: Depression increases the risk of tobacco, alcohol, and illicit drug use and may contribute to inadequate prenatal care. In addition, it increases the risk of self-injurious and suicidal behavior. Several studies have found an association between depression during pregnancy and preterm delivery, lower birth weight, smaller head circumference, low Apgar scores, and postpartum depression (Bloch et al., 2006; Cohen & Nonacs, 2005). Depression can lead to reduced interaction and irritability toward the child (Halbreich, 2005). In a study of women enrolled in Kaiser Permanente Northwest, approximately half of women with clinically diagnosed perinatal depression experienced depression in the 39 weeks before pregnancy, highlighting the need for identification and treatment of depression among nonpregnant women of reproductive age (Dietz et al., 2007).

Causes of low birth weight deliveries: Epidemiological data have shown an association between children with a low birth weight and an increased risk to develop several metabolic, cardiovascular, and behavioral problems in later life. This programming phenomenon, known as the "fetal origins of adult diseases" (FOAD), proposes that these disorders are derived from fetal adaptations due to intra-uterine disturbances. The FOAD hypothesis has been tested in animal models using maternal under-nutrition, and stress during early-, mid-, or late-trimester or throughout pregnancy. These in-utero stressors altered birth weight, neuroendocrine responses, immune functions, cognitive function, and pain inducing behavior. Furthermore, cardiovascular and metabolic disorders such as hypertension, hyperglycemia, hyperinsulinemia occur and persist throughout life (Barker, 1995).

Diabetes affects 9.3% of women of childbearing age. A threefold increase in the prevalence of birth defects among infants of women with type 1 and type 2 diabetes is substantially reduced through proper management of diabetes.

Exposure to alcohol is one of the leading preventable causes of birth defects, mental retardation, and neurodevelopmental disorders; alcohol misuse can cause harm to a fetus before a woman realizes that she is pregnant (American Academy of Pediatrics, 2000). In the 2004 BRFSS, 53.9% of preconception women and 10.7% of pregnant women surveyed reported having used alcohol in the past month. Numerous studies have documented the effects of alcohol use during pregnancy, including the effects of exposure during the first trimester, a critical period of development for the central nervous system in the embryo and fetus. Studies have confirmed that early gestational exposure to alcohol results in the malformed and misshapen facial features characteristic of fetal alcohol syndrome (FAS). Ethanol exposure during the embryonic period—the first 3 to 8 weeks of gestation— is particularly damaging (Coles, 1994; Moore, 1988).

Hepatitis B: Prevention of hepatitis B infection through inoculations in women of childbearing age prevents transmission to their infants and eliminates risks to the women themselves.

HIV/AIDS: Approximately one-third of preconception and pregnant women surveyed in the United States in the 2004 Behavioral Risk Factor Surveillance System (BRFSS) were not aware of methods to prevent mother-to-child HIV/AIDS transmission. If HIV infection is identified before conception, timely antiretroviral treatment can be given to help prevent mother-to-child transmission.

Hypothyroidism affects 1.4% of women of childbearing age; prior to conception, dosages of thyroxine need to be adjusted for proper neurologic development of the fetus.

Inadequate nutrition: Adequate nutrition both pre- and postnatally, is crucial for brain growth. From the 2004 BRFSS, 74.9% of preconception women did not report consuming the recommended 5 servings of fruits and vegetables per day (Anderson, Ebrahim, Floyd, & Atrash, 2006). Low BMI (<19.8 BMI) may reflect chronic nutritional deficiency and is associated with intrauterine growth retardation, preterm birth, and iron deficiency anemia (Siega-Riz & Laraia, 2006).

Isolated pregnancy: Expectant mothers who shoulder most of the burden of running a household or who lack a close relationship with a husband or partner may experience less nutritional provisioning by others and a greater workload, both of which could contribute to fewer net calories per day and, by extension, reduced maternal and fetal weight gain (Hobel, Goldstein, & Barrett, 2008). Feldman, Dunkel-Schetter, Sandman, & Wadhwa (2000) found that social support (and other variables) accounted for 31% of the variance in fetal growth in their study (after controlling for gestational age). Women who had multiple types of social support from different sources, in fact, had infants with the highest birth weight. On the basis of these results and an extensive review of the literature on social support and birth weight, they concluded that social support may promote higher birth weights.

Isotretinoins (e.g., Accutane) are used to treat acne; however, when used during pregnancy isotretinoins can result in miscarriage and birth defects (e.g., craniofacial, cardiac, thymic, and central nervous system malformations) and developmental delay even after only one dose.

Maternal smoking during pregnancy is associated with preterm birth, low birth weight, and other adverse perinatal outcomes that can be prevented if a woman stops smoking before or during early pregnancy. In the 2004 BRFSS, 19.5% of preconception women and 8.4% of pregnant women smoked (Anderson, Ebrahim, Floyd, & Atrash, 2006). Counseling should commence before pregnancy occurs.

Noise: Noise is an environmental exposure that may cause hearing loss and other health problems in a fetus. The cochlea is fully developed by 24 weeks gestation and blink-startle responses to loud noises are consistently present by 28 weeks gestation. Therefore the acoustic pathways of the central nervous system are mature enough to be damaged. Sound is easily transmitted into the uterine environment and experienced by the fetus. Some studies have found associations between pregnant women who were exposed to occupational noise (85 to 95 dB) and higher risk of preterm delivery as well as decreased birth weight and high-frequency hearing loss in their children (American Academy of Pediatrics, 1997).

Obesity is associated with adverse reproductive health outcomes including infertility, neural tube defects, preterm delivery, diabetes, cesarean delivery, prolonged labor, and hypertensive and thromboembolic disease. Appropriate weight loss and nutritional intake before pregnancy reduces these risks (Siega-Riz & Laraia, 2006). Nearly one-fifth of 2004 BRFSS preconception women were obese and two-fifths were overweight.

Oral anticoagulants: Warfarin has been shown to be a teratogen (an agent that can produce structural or functional abnormalities in a developing embryo or fetus). Medications can be changed to a nonteratogenic anticoagulant before conception.

Phenylketonuria (PKU): Women diagnosed as infants with PKU have an increased risk for delivering infants with mental retardation or birth defects; however, this can be prevented when mothers adhere to a low-phenylalanine diet before conception and throughout pregnancy.

Prolonged stress: Alleviating prolonged stress before and during of pregnancy has been shown to increase the chances of a positive pregnancy. Recent research indicates that psychological and physiological stress play a possible role in adverse birth outcomes. Chronic psychological or biologic stress can weaken the immune system and interrupt the modulation of the inflammatory response (Culhane, Elo, & Irma 2005). Women who enter pregnancy with immune system problems and an oversensitive inflammatory response may be more susceptible to pregnancy complications, including preterm birth (Lu, Tache, Kotelchuck, & Halfon, 2003; McEwen, 1998). Prenatal stress also predicts fearfulness in children. This effect persisted even after controlling for maternal education and psychological state, exposures to medications and substances during pregnancy, and birth outcomes. Prenatal stress also accounts for 17% of changes in cognitive ability. Relationship strain with the partner accounted for 73.5% and 75.0% of the prenatal stress-related variance on infant cognitive and fearfulness scores, respectively (Bergman, Sarkar, O'Connor, Modi, & Glover, 2007). It has also been found that the availability of social supports acts as a buffer against pregnancy complications associated with daily life stress and emotional distress (Norbeck & Tilden, 1983). In a Russian study, perceived stress—living in crowded or shared housing and excessive paternal drinking—were associated with decreased birth weight (Grjibovski et al., 2004; Pritchard & Teo, 1998).

Rubella: Vaccination against rubella prior to conception prevents congenital rubella syndrome.

Sexually transmitted infections (STIs), such as *Chlamydia trachomatis* and *Neisseria gonorrhoeae*, have been strongly associated with ectopic pregnancy, infertility, and chronic pelvic pain. STIs during pregnancy might result in fetal death or substantial physical and developmental disabilities, including mental retardation and blindness. Early screening and treatment can prevent these adverse outcomes.

Tetracycline: The antibiotic tetracycline if taken during the second and third trimesters can damage the fetal kidneys. The period of greatest sensitivity to most teratogenic exposures is the period from 18 to 60 days postconception, which is approximately 4.5–11 weeks after the last menstrual period. Exposures after this period usually do not result in structural anomalies, although there are exceptions. Rather, exposures during the fetal period (after 60 days postconception) typically result in growth restriction or functional disorders of the central nervous system, kidneys, or other organs (Rutledge, 1997).

Program for Infant/ Toddler Care (PITC) Philosophy and Recommendations

PITC PHILOSOPHY

At the heart of the Program for Infant/Toddler Care is a commitment to care for infants and toddlers that respects the differing cultures, lifestyles, preferences, abilities, learning styles, and needs of the children and families served. Therefore, the Program for Infant/Toddler Care follows an approach that is responsive to what the infants and toddlers and their families bring to care and emphasizes relationship-based implementation strategies. The positions advocated by PITC are based on sound child development and family research, leading to the following working assumptions:

- Families need to be partners in care. Programs should seek out families' beliefs, values, practices, and child-rearing strategies and include them in the program's caregiving practices whenever possible.
- Young children are unique individuals with varying temperaments, rates of development, and interests. These individual differences should be identified and strategies appropriate to each child's unique needs incorporated into child-care practice.
- Young children are curious, motivated learners and also dependent upon adults for nurturance, support, and guidance. They need to be both respected as learners and protected in their vulnerability. Therefore, planning for a child's care in the program is a shared experience including families and program staff and is individualized for children by
  - » welcoming family and cultural practices, including home language, as a part of the child-care experience;

> » providing infants close and responsive relationships with caregivers in intimate settings;
> » designing safe, interesting, and developmentally appropriate environments;
> » giving infants uninterrupted time to explore; and
> » interacting with infants during caregiving routines and throughout the day in ways that physically, emotionally, socially, and intellectually support their initiations in discovery and learning.

Source: Developed by J. Ronald Lally & Peter Mangione. © 2006 WestEd, The Program for Infant/Toddler Care. The above section may be reproduced for educational purposes.

SIX PROGRAM POLICIES THAT ANCHOR PITC WORK

Primary Care: In a primary care system, each child is assigned to one special caregiver who is principally responsible for that child's care. When children spend a longer day in care than their primary caregiver, a second caregiver is assigned to the primary role. Each child should have a special caregiver assigned to him or her at all times during the child-care day. Teaming is also important. Primary care works best when caregivers team up and support each other and provide a back-up base for security for each other's primary care children. Primary care does not mean exclusive care. It means, however, that all parties know who has primary responsibility for each child.

Small Groups: Every major research study on infant and toddler care has shown that small group size *and* good ratios are key components of quality care. PITC recommends primary care ratios of 1:3 or 1:4 in groups of 6 to 12 children, depending on the age. The guiding principle is the younger the child, the smaller the group. Small groups facilitate the provision of personalized care that infants and toddlers need, supporting peaceful exchanges, freedom and safety to move and explore, and the development of intimate relationships.

Continuity: Continuity of care is the third key to providing the deep connections that infants and toddlers need for quality child care. Programs that incorporate the concept of continuity of care keep primary caregivers and children together throughout the 3 years of infancy period, or for the time during that period of the child's enrollment in care.

Individualized Care: Following children's unique rhythms and styles promotes well-being and a healthy sense of self. It's important not to make a child feel bad about him- or herself because of biological rhythms or needs that are different from those of other children. Responding promptly to children's individual needs supports their growing ability to self-regulate, that is, to function independently in personal and social contexts. The program adapts to the child, rather than vice versa, and the child gets the message that he or she is important, that her/his needs will be met, and that his/her choices, preferences, and impulses are respected.

Cultural Continuity: Children develop a sense of who they are and what is important within the context of culture. Traditionally, it has been the child's family and cultural community that have been responsible for the transmission of values, expectations, and ways of doing things, especially during the early years of life. As more children enter child care during the tender years of infancy, questions of their cultural identity and sense of belonging in their own families are raised. Consistency of care between home and child care, always important for the very young, becomes even more so when the infant or toddler is cared for in the context of cultural practices different from that of the child's family. Because of the important role of culture in development, caregivers who serve families from diverse backgrounds need to

1. heighten their understanding of the importance of culture in the lives of infants;
2. develop cultural competencies;
3. acknowledge and respect cultural differences, and;
4. learn to be open and responsive to, and willing to negotiate with families about, child-rearing practices.

In this way, families and caregivers, working together, can facilitate the optimal development of each child.

Inclusion of Children with Special Needs: Inclusion means making the benefits of high quality care available to all infants through appropriate accommodation and support in order for the child to have full active program participation. Issues already embraced by the PITC—a relationship-based approach to the provision of care that is individualized and responsive to the child's cues and desires to learn—are equally important for children with disabilities or other special needs. Infants who have responsive, enduring relationships develop emotional security, which gives them the foundation for becoming socially competent and resilient. Infants who have individualized care are allowed to learn and grow in their own way and at their own pace.

PITC RECOMMENDATIONS FOR GROUP SIZE, RATIOS, AND AMOUNT OF SPACE

Same-Age Groups

Group	Age	Total Group Size	Square Feet Per Group	Ratios
Young Infants	Birth–8 months	6	350	1:3
Mobile Infants	6–18 months	9	500	1:3
Older Infants	16–36 months	12	600	1:4

Mixed-Age Groups

Age	Total Group Size	Square Feet Per Group	Ratio
Birth–36+ months	8	600	1:4

Note: The space guidelines represent recommended standards of square footage per group; the amounts shown do not include space used for entrance areas, hallways, diapering areas, or napping areas.

Another acceptable grouping option is the Early Head Start program model with ratios of 1:4 in a group size of 8 for children from 0–36 months of age. This arrangement supports continuity of care as ratios and group size remain constant for the first 3 years of life. Groups may be of same-age or mixed-age children.

PITC Recommendations for Creating Small, Self-Contained Groups

1. Create separate groups of children in rooms with floor-to-ceiling walls.
2. Assign no more than 6 to 12 children to a room, depending upon the age of the children.
3. Maintain age-appropriate ratios of 3 or 4 children to a primary caregiver throughout the day.
4. Provide facilities for caregiving activities including feeding, toileting, and sleeping in each room.
5. Include a self-contained outdoor play space for each group with direct access from the room.

Source: Developed by Sheila Signer and Alicia Tuesta. © 2004 WestEd, The Program for Infant/Toddler Care. May be reproduced for educational purposes.

Health-Care Services During Pregnancy Recommended by the U.S. Department of Health and Human Services

Screening, immunization, and counseling events are recommended for all pregnant women at 11 different contact points as pregnancy advances. If these recommendations were heeded, pregnancy outcomes for American mothers and their babies would be greatly improved.

Preconception Visit	Visit 1** 6–8 weeks	Visit 2 10–12 weeks	Visit 3 16–18 weeks	Visit 4 22 weeks
Event: Screening Maneuvers				
Risk profiles	Risk profiles	Weight	Weight	Weight
Height and weight/BMI	GC/Chlamydia	Blood pressure	Blood pressure	Blood pressure
Blood pressure	Height and weight/BMI	Fetal aneuploidy screening	Depression	Fetal heart tones
History and physical	Blood pressure	Fetal heart tones	Fetal aneuploidy screening	Fundal height
Cholesterol and HDL	History and physical*		Fetal heart tones	
Cervical cancer screening	Rubella		OB ultrasound (optional)	
Rubella/Rubeola	Varicella		Fundal height	
Varicella	Domestic violence			
Domestic violence	Depression			
Depression	CBC			
	ABO/Rh/Ab			
	Syphilis			
	Urine culture			
	HIV			
	[Blood lead screening]			
	[VBAC]			
	Viral hepatitis			

116

Preconception Visit	Visit 1** 6–8 weeks	Visit 2 10–12 weeks	Visit 3 16–18 weeks	Visit 4 22 weeks
Event: Counseling Education Intervention				
Preterm labor education and prevention	Preterm labor education and prevention	Preterm labor education and prevention	Preterm labor education and prevention	Preterm labor education and prevention
Substance use	Prenatal and lifestyle education	Prenatal and lifestyle education	Prenatal and lifestyle education	Prenatal and lifestyle education
Nutrition and weight	Physical activity	Fetal growth	Follow-up of modifiable risk factors	Follow-up of modifiable risk factors
Domestic violence	Nutrition	Review lab results from Visit 1	Physiology of pregnancy	Classes
List of medications, herbal supplements, vitamins	Follow-up of modifiable risk factors	Breastfeeding	Second trimester growth	Family issues
Accurate recording of menstrual dates	Nausea and vomiting	Nausea and vomiting	Quickening	Length of stay
	Warning signs	Physiology of pregnancy		GDM
	Course of care	Follow-up of modifiable risk factors		[RhoGAM]
	Physiology of pregnancy			
	Discuss fetal aneuploidy screening			
Event: Immunization and Chemoprophylaxis				
Tetanus booster	Tetanus booster		[Progesterone]	
Rubella/MMR	Nutritional supplements			
[Varicella/VZIG]	Influenza			
Hepatitis B vaccine	[Varicella/ VZIG]***			
Folic acid supplement	Pertussis			

[Bracketed] items refer to high-risk groups only.

*It is acceptable for the history and physical and laboratory tests listed under Visit 1 to be deferred to Visit 2 with the agreement of both the patient and the provider.

** Should also include all subjects listed for the preconception visit if none occurred.

*** Administration of the Varicella vaccine during pregnancy is contraindicated.

Abbreviations: Ab, antibody; Ag, antigen; ABO, blood group system; BMI, body mass index; CBC, complete blood count; CPR, cardiopulmonary resuscitation; GC, gonococci; GDM, gestational diabetes mellitus; HDL, high density lipoprotein; HIV, human immunodeficiency virus; MMR, measles/mumps/rubella; OB, obstetrics; RhoGAM, Rho(D) immune globulin; VBAC, vaginal birth after cesarean; VZIG, Varicella zoster immune globulin

Source: National Guideline Clearinghouse. (2007). *National Guidelines for Prenatal Visits.* Retrieved from http://www.guidelines.gov/content.aspx?id=24138&search=prenatal

Visit 5 28 weeks	Visit 6 32 weeks	Visit 7 36 weeks	Visit 8–11 38–41 weeks
Event: Screening Maneuvers			
Preterm labor risk Weight Blood pressure Depression Fetal heart tones Fundal height GDM Domestic abuse [Rh antibody status] [Hepatitis B surface Ag] [GC/Chlamydia]	Weight Blood pressure Fetal heart tones Fundal height	Weight Blood pressure Fetal heart tones Fundal height Cervix exam Confirm fetal position Culture for group B streptococcus	Weight Blood pressure Fetal heart tones Fundal height Cervix exam
Event: Counseling Education Intervention			
Psychosocial risk factors Preterm labor education and prevention Prenatal and lifestyle education Follow-up modifiable risk factors Work Physiology of pregnancy Preregistration Fetal growth Awareness of fetal movement	Preterm labor education and prevention Prenatal and lifestyle education Follow-up of modifiable risk factors Travel Contraception Sexuality Pediatric care Episiotomy Labor and delivery issues Warning signs/pregnancy-induced hypertension [VBAC]	Prenatal and lifestyle education Follow-up of modifiable risk factors Postpartum care Management of late pregnancy symptoms Contraception When to call provider Discussion of postpartum depression	Prenatal and lifestyle education Follow-up of modifiable risk factors Postpartum vaccinations Infant CPR Post-term management Labor and delivery update
Event: Immunization and Chemoprophylaxi			
[ABO/Rh/Ab] [RhoGAM]			

[Bracketed] items refer to high-risk groups only.

*It is acceptable for the history and physical and laboratory tests listed under Visit 1 to be deferred to Visit 2 with the agreement of both the patient and the provider.

** Should also include all subjects listed for the preconception visit if none occurred.

*** Administration of the Varicella vaccine during pregnancy is contraindicated.

Abbreviations: Ab, antibody; Ag, antigen; ABO, blood group system; BMI, body mass index; CBC, complete blood count; CPR, cardiopulmonary resuscitation; GC, gonococci; GDM, gestational diabetes mellitus; HDL, high density lipoprotein; HIV, human immunodeficiency virus; MMR, measles/mumps/rubella; OB, obstetrics; RhoGAM, Rho(D) immune globulin; VBAC, vaginal birth after cesarean; VZIG, Varicella zoster immune globulin

Source: National Guideline Clearinghouse. (2007). *National Guidelines for Prenatal Visits.* Retrieved from http://www.guidelines.gov/content.aspx?id=24138&search=prenatal

A Sample of Paid-Leave Policies in Other Countries

CANADA

- Maternity benefits are payable to the natural mother in the period surrounding the birth of a child and may start from 8 weeks before the expected date of birth to the week of actual delivery. Fifteen weeks of maternity benefits are allowed after a 2-week waiting period and can be collected within 17 weeks of the actual week of confinement or week of expected confinement, whichever is later. However, the 17-week limit can be extended and payments delayed for every week a baby is confined to the hospital for up to 52 weeks following the week of the child's birth. It may also be possible to receive sickness benefits in addition to the maximum weeks of maternity benefits should an employee be unable to work because of complications due to pregnancy or childbirth or by reason of an unrelated illness. Benefits usually cover 55% of a claimant's weekly insurable earnings to a maximum of $413 per week.

References

Human Resources and Skills Development Canada. (2010). *Work and family provisions in Canadian collective agreements*: Maternity. Ottawa, Canada: Treasury Board of Canada Secretariat.

- In 2006, the Canadian province of Quebec introduced a new parental leave policy, one that is substantially different from those found in the rest of Canada (Tremblay, 2009). In addition to maternity leave, it includes a paternity leave that is nontransferable to the mother, as well as a 1-year paid parental leave that can be shared between the parents. The program offers maternity leave and allows both parents to benefit from a flexible parental leave that can last up to 1 year and pay 55% or 75% of the salary depending on which of the two options is chosen (Doucet, McKay, &

Tremblay, 2009; Tremblay, 2009). It also offers a 3-week (75% wage replacement) or 5-week (55% wage replacement) period of paid paternity leave that is nontransferable to the mother. This nontransferable paternity leave and the possibility to share the parental leave are clearly intended to encourage men to participate fully in parental responsibilities when the children are very young. The presumption is that after this experience, men would participate more in the child's education when he or she is older (Conseil de la Famille et de l'Enfance, 2008; Tanaka & Waldfogel, 2007) and that this would further benefit child development in both the short and long term (Driessen, Smit, & Sleegers, 2005) and in work-life balance (Marshall, 2008).

References

Conseil de la Famille et de l'Enfance. (2008). *L'engagement des pères*. Rapport 2007–2008. Québec: Conseil de la Famille et de l'Enfance.

Doucet, A., McKay, L., & Tremblay, D. G. (2009). Parental leave in Canada and Québec: How to explain the different routes taken? In P. Moss & S. Kamerman (Eds.), *The politics of parental leave policies* (pp. 33–51). Bristol, UK: Policy Press.

Driessen, G., Smit, F., & Sleegers, P. (2005). Parental involvement and educational achievement. *British Educational Research Journal, 31*(4), 509–532.

Marshall, K. (2008). Fathers' use of paid parental leave. *Perspectives, 9*(6), 5–14.

Tanaka, S., & Waldfogel, J. (2007). Effects of parental leave and work hours on fathers' involvement with their babies. *Community, Work & Family, 10*(4), 409–426.

Tremblay, D. G. (2009). Quebec's policies for work-family balance: A model for Canada? In M. Cohen & J. Pulkingham (Eds.), *Public policy for women. The state, income security and labour market issues* (pp. 271–290). Toronto: University of Toronto Press.

- In 2001, parental leave was extended to 35 weeks, the 2-week waiting period was eliminated for the second parent (to encourage participation), the required number of hours worked were reduced from 700 to 600, making it easier for women working part time or in unstable jobs to qualify. It also made it easier for mothers of very young children to work part time by allowing them to retain earnings up to the equivalent of 25% of benefits.

- The provinces still determine the length of leave for workers within their jurisdictions, but most follow the pattern established within the Canada Labor Code. All parents with access to federal unemployment legislation have the right to paid leave of equivalent length and the same terms no matter where they live.

- Canada's program does include all but the self-employed, but only those who have met the (fairly stringent) work requirements for the previous year. Although it nominally includes fathers, the low rate of remuneration (55% or a ceiling of 447 Canadian dollars a week) reduces the incentive for fathers to participate. There is no special part set aside exclusively for fathers (a "daddy quota"). Thus there is little incentive for men to take a significant share.

References

Mahon, R., & Brennan, D. (2012). Federalism and the "New Politics" of welfare development: Childcare and parental leave in Australia and Canada. *Publius*, *42*, 2–18.

- The Quebec parental leave program reflects a stronger commitment to gender equality. In addition to the elimination of the 2-week waiting period for the "first parent," the Quebec plan includes a 5-week paternity benefit or "daddy quota" and offers a higher rate of remuneration (75% to a maximum of $57,000) for 7 weeks. It also includes the self-employed. These features have had an impact not only on eligibility levels for women (77% versus 62% in the rest of Canada) but also on fathers' participation rates. Thus, in 2006, 56% of eligible Quebec fathers claimed leave benefits versus 10% of those in the rest of Canada (Marshall, 2008).

References

Marshall, K. (2008). Fathers' use of paid parental leave. *Perspectives*, *9*(6), 5–14.

FRANCE

- Sixteen weeks of maternity leave, 11 days of paternity leave, and 10 weeks of adoption leave, all paid at the parent's usual wage rate. These leaves are extended when there are multiple births or adoptions, or if the family has a total of at least three children.
- New fathers in France can use 11 consecutive days of fully-paid paternity leave. With twins (or more), paternity leave is extended to 18 days. An additional 3 days of "family leave" can also be added for a total of 14 or 21 days. The cash benefit equals the maximum benefit covered under social security. Employers may top off these benefits for individuals with higher salaries.
- During maternity, paternity, and adoption leaves, parents receive an allowance from their local sickness insurance funds if they have been registered and contributing for at least 10 months before the date of birth

or adoption. These allowances amount to 100% of their usual after-taxes salary, within the upper and lower boundaries of €8.39 and €71.80 per day. Upon their return to work, new parents are guaranteed their previous position or a similar one. In 2007, almost all (97%) of mothers availed themselves of maternity leaves, as did two-thirds of fathers. Parents may choose to take the leave at the same time or sequentially.

- Although the leave is income-tested, about 90% of families with children are eligible. The duration of the leave is up to 3 years and it can be extended by one year in case of sickness, accident, or handicap of the child. The leave can be taken as a full-time or part-time leave from work (between 16 and 32 hours per week).
- Within the first 3 years of a child's birth or adoption, parents can take full- or part-time leave for home-based childcare, while receiving flat-rate payments from the social insurance system.
- As of January 1, 2004, new parents in France are entitled to claim a Paje allowance. This bonus following birth or adoption includes a baby bonus, a basic children's allowance due until the child's third birthday, a worker occupation choice supplement, and finally a choice of child-care mode supplement.
- Eight weeks of the maternity leave are compulsory, of which at least 6 weeks must be taken after childbirth.
- There are compulsory prenatal and postnatal medical examinations.
- Medical care is covered as well. Benefits are payable in case of adoption and correspond to those for the postnatal period, with additional leave granted when the adoption raises the number of children in the household to three or higher (Fagnani & Boyer, 2008).

References

Fagnani, J., & Boyer, D. (2008). France. In P. Moss & M. Korintus (Eds.), *International review of leave policies and related research* (pp. 200–206). London: Department for Business Enterprise & Regulatory Reform.

Government of France. (2009). *Fiches prattiques: Maternité/paternité/adoption* [Prattic cards: Maternity/paternity/adoption]. Paris: Ministry of Labor Solidarity, Family, and Social Relation.

Appelbaum, E., & Milkman, R. (2011, January 19). Paid family leave pays off in California. *Harvard Business Review*. Retrieved from http://blogs.hbr.org/research/2011/01/paid-family-leave-pays-off-in.html

International Labour Organization. (2010). *Maternity protection database*. Retrieved from http://www.ilo.org/dyn/travail/travmain.home

Nicholas, M. (2008). Prestation d'accueil du jeune enfant: quelques éléments d'appréciation des résultats de l'évaluation, *Informations sociales, 150*, 118–126. OECD.

Organisation for Economic Co-operation and Development. (2009). *OECD Family Database*. Retrieved from http://www.oecd.org/document/4/0,3746, en_2649_34819_37836996_1_1_1_1,00.html

GERMANY

- Parents receive benefits during both maternity and parental leave.
- During maternity leave, women are eligible for a maternity allowance ("Mutterschaftsgeld") if they have been enrolled in a statutory insurance program for at least 12 weeks during the period between 10 months and 4 months before the child's expected birth date. Insurance enrollment is available to women who are employed, receiving unemployment benefits, or in an educational program. The Mutterschaftsgeld pays the woman her full usual after-tax wages, up to €13 per day. If her usual wages are above €13 per day, the remainder is paid by her employer.
- Parents taking parental leave receive a parental allowance ("Elterngeld," formerly known as "Erziehungsgeld") for 12 months of parental leave per family at a rate of 67% of their usual salary. Parents may also claim the childrearing benefit at half the usual rate for twice the usual length.
- Two additional months of benefits are available exclusively for the father's use, but if he does not use them they are not deducted from the family's 12-month benefit. Therefore, German families have 14 months of benefit to share, with 2 months reserved for the father's use.
- German parents have the right to parental leave until the child's third birthday. They must take the first 2 years immediately after the child's birth or adoption and may postpone the third until any time before the child's eighth birthday.
- Beyond these 14 months of parental leave, all German employees with home-care responsibilities have the right to request part-time work schedules, and employees at firms that employ more than 15 workers are guaranteed the right to such a schedule. However, only full-time workers have the right to return to their old position when they are finished taking parental leave. Employees who were working part-time schedules before parental leave have no such guarantee.

References

Department for Business Enterprise & Regulatory Reform. (2007). *International*

review of leave policies and related research. London: Department for Business
Enterprise & Regulatory Reform.

European Foundation for the Improvement of Living and Working Conditions.
(2009). *Foundation findings: Childcare services in Europe.* Dublin: European
Foundation for the Improvement of Living and Working Conditions.

Honekamp, I. (2008). Family policy in Germany: Appraisal and assessment. *Journal of Family History, 33*(4), 452–464.

ITALY

- Italian child-based leave consists of maternity and parental leave; no
  separate paternity leave exists. Maternity leave lasts for 5 months, paid at
  80% of a mother's usual salary.

- Parental leave lasts for 6 months per parent (with a maximum of 11
  months per child). During 6 of those 11 months, parents receive benefits
  amounting to 30% of their usual salary. Thus, if a family uses all of their
  allotted leave, they will have 11 months of paid leave and 5 months of
  unpaid leave.

- During maternity leave, employed mothers who are registered with
  the National Social Security Institute (Istituto Nazionale Previdenza
  Sociale [INPS]) receive 80% of their usual salary. There are no tenure
  requirements for this benefit, and it is available to part-time workers as
  well as full-time workers. The INPS also pays women who are registered
  but ineligible for maternity pay due to unemployment or irregular
  schedules at a flat rate of €283 per month (in 2007).

- Mothers who have no employment record and thus are not registered with
  the INPS receive a one-time government assistance grant of €1,747.

- Some flexibility exists for parents scheduling parental leave. Parents may
  take it simultaneously or separately. Parental leave can also be taken
  any time before the child's eighth birthday (sixth birthday in the case of
  adoption) and as soon as the end of maternity leave (for mothers) or the
  child's birth. However, INPS will only pay benefits during parental leave if
  it is taken within the first 3 years of the child's life.

- Italian mothers have the right to, and must take, 5 months of maternity
  leave: 2 prenatal months and 3 postnatal months. However, with
  permission from their doctors, a healthy pregnant woman can postpone
  maternity leave by 1 month and thus have 4 months of leave after the
  child's birth. Less healthy women may take their full pregnancy terms as
  maternity leave if their doctors feel that their medical histories put their
  pregnancies in risk.

References

Anxo, D., Fagan, C., Letablier, M.-T., Perraudin, C., & Smith, M. (2007). European foundation for the improvement of living and working conditions, part-time work and work–life balance in European companies: Establishment survey on working time 2004–2005. Luxembourg: Office for Official Publications of the European Communities.

European Foundation for the Improvement of Living and Working Conditions. (2007). *Parental leave in European companies: Establishment survey on working time 2004–2005*. Retrieved from http://www.eurofound.europa.eu/pubdocs/2006/87/en/1/ef0687en.pdf

Fagan, C., & Hebson, G. (2006). "Making work pay" debates from a gender perspective: A comparative review of some recent policy reforms in thirty European countries. Luxembourg: Office for Official Publications of the European Communities.

Istituto Nazionale Previdenza Sociale (2007). *Indennità di Maternità, Congedo Parentale*. Rome: Author.

SWEDEN

- Families receive 480 calendar days of paid leave. If a two-parent family were to take all possible leave, they would have a total of 480 days of paid leave and 664 calendar days (approximately 22 months) of unpaid leave, as well as the right to work part-time for 6.5 years each.
- Parents have substantial timing flexibility; they may take their leave either full time or part time, simultaneously or sequentially, and either continuously or in up to 3 blocks of time per year. The first 480 calendar days taken by a family are paid; if they have not taken all 480 of these days before their child is 18 months old, they may continue to take them until the child's eighth birthday or until the end of the child's first year of school (whichever is sooner), but parents may not take more than those 480 calendar days. Until the end of the child's first year of school or his or her eighth birthday, all parents may also reduce their working hours (and salary) by 25%.
- The income-replacement level is normally 80% of previous earnings up to a relatively high ceiling of earnings.
- Parental leave benefits are financed through general taxes with no direct costs to employers.
- All parents permanently residing in the country are entitled to parental leave benefits. Earnings-related benefits apply to parents who had earnings during the 8 months before childbirth. Also, unemployed parents can claim earnings-related benefits if they can prove previous employment

and income. Each parent is entitled to parental-leave benefits based on his or her own individual earnings. The only requirement is that parents do not take leave simultaneously.

- In Sweden, the replacement rate from a previous birth interval can be claimed also for a younger sibling if the next child is born within 30 months. This so called "speed premium" in the benefit system is aimed at supporting a sufficient allowance level subsequent to higher-order births, especially in situations when the mother may have reduced her work hours after the birth of the first child.

References

Duvander, A. Z. (2008). *Family policy in Sweden: An overview* (Social insurance report 2008: 15). Stockholm: Swedish Social Insurance Agency.

Government Offices of Sweden. (2009). *More time for young children and parental benefit*. Information brochures from the Ministry of Health and Social Affairs.

Sundström, M. & Duvander, A. Z. (2002). Gender division of childcare and the sharing of parental leave among new parents in Sweden, *European Sociological Review, 18*, 433–447.

Swedish Institute. (2007). *Gender equality in Sweden: Fact Sheet 82q*. Stockholm: Swedish Institute.

NORWAY

- Parents are given the choice between two specific leave programs: 56 weeks (before 2009: 52 weeks) with 80% wage compensation or 46 weeks (before 2009: 42 weeks) with 100% wage compensation. Most parents choose the former option.
- Eligibility for parental-leave benefits requires employment during 6 of the last 10 months prior to childbearing. Norwegian mothers who are not entitled to leave benefits instead receive a one-time, tax-free cash payment at childbirth that in 1995 was equivalent to €3,200. Fathers' rights to benefits in Norway were, until 2000, totally based on mothers' eligibility, even when the father had himself been employed. From 2000, the Norwegian policy changed and fathers may now use parental benefits based on their own eligibility, except for the fathers' quota, which a father cannot use if the mother is not eligible for parental leave. In practice, this change did not affect behavior much, as fathers' leave beyond the quota requires that the mother is not at home with the family, which she normally is if she is not eligible for leave.

- The income-replacement level is normally 80% of previous earnings up to a relatively high ceiling of earnings.
- Parental-leave benefits are financed through general taxes with no direct costs to employers.

References

Aassve, A., & Lappegård, T. (2009). Childcare cash benefits and fertility timing in Norway. *European Journal of Population, 25,* 67–88.

Lappegård, T. (2008). Changing the gender balance in caring: Fatherhood and the division of parental leave in Norway, *Population Research and Policy Review, 27,* 139–159.

Ministry of Children and Family Affairs (1996). *Public transfers to families with children* (Norwegian official report 13). Olso, Norway: Author.

Organisation for Economic Cooperation and Development (2007). Babies and bosses: Reconciling work and family life—A synthesis of findings for OECD Countries. Paris: OECD Publishing.

Norwegian Labour and Welfare Administration. (2009). *Parental benefit on birth.* Retrieved from http://www.nav.no/805369034.cms

Well-Baby Care Services in Other Countries

Financing

Several countries (Sweden, France, Australia) use separate, public nurse-based maternal- and child-health (MCH) systems to provide immunizations and/ or well-child care elements of prevention, guidance, and counseling. In these countries, well-child care is largely publicly financed with virtually no cost sharing (e.g., premiums, deductibles, or copayments). In France, maternal and child preventive health care, education, and social and financial support are encompassed in the Protection Maternelle et Infantile (PMI). The PMI started after World War II to combat infant mortality and morbidity by providing "protection for all" and offering preventive health care with no cost to all children younger than 6 years. Parents who choose not to receive these services through the PMI may pay some costs for this care in the private sector. Also in France, parents may pay a share of cost if well-child care is received from private physicians.

Cost sharing varies by country. In Japan, there is variable cost sharing depending on the scope of employer coverage. Whereas no costs apply to primary care in England, Sweden, Germany, and Spain, some cost sharing may apply to acute and chronic primary care services in Australia and France, depending on the nature of the child's medical insurance and, in Australia, on whether the parent selects a private plan to supplement publicly financed services for the child.

Services

Some countries such as Sweden and England have interdisciplinary child health-care "teams" that provide components of well-child care. The state of Victoria has the most developed MCH system in Australia. Virtually all well-child care including immunizations, anticipatory guidance and counseling, and developmental surveillance is delivered by nurses from geographically based maternal- and child-health centers. Home nursing services supplement the MCH nurse activities offered through these centers. Pediatricians serve a specialty role and provide some developmental screening for children identified by the MCH nurses or a child's general-practice physician (providing acute and chronic care) with a specific concern. Examples of countries with distinct responsibilities for well-child care among MCH nurses and physicians include France and the Netherlands. In Japan, some prefectures use public health nurses to provide well-child care, whereas in other prefectures it is a responsibility of general practice physicians. In contrast, well-child care is provided by general practice physicians and pediatricians in Germany and general practice physicians in Canada. Although French PMIs offer preventive services universally, most children see private practice pediatricians for preventive care; PMIs provide preventive services largely to children in lower-income households. In France, public preschools (*école maternelle*) provide an additional site of health care for young children.

References

Kuo, A., Inkelas, M., Lotstein, D., Samson, K., Schor, E., & Halfon, N. (2006). Rethinking well-child care in the United States: An international comparison. *Pediatrics, 118(4),* 1692–1702.

Credentialing, Certification, and Training

Child Care Aware America/National Association of Child Care Resource and Referral Agencies (NACCRRA) Recommended Credential and Certification Benchmarks

- Center directors are required to have a bachelor's degree or higher in early childhood education or a related field.
- Lead teachers are required to have a Child Development Associate (CDA) credential or an associate degree in early childhood education or related field.
- Lead teachers are required to have initial training, including orientation training and training in fire safety and other health and safety issues. At least one staff member who is certified in first aid and CPR must be present when children are in care.
- Lead teachers are required to have 24 hours or more of annual training.
- A comprehensive background check is required for child-care providers.

Program for Infant/Toddler Care (PITC) Recommended Content for Training of Infant/Toddler Teachers

The content is divided into four modules:

Module I addresses social-emotional growth and socialization of infants and toddlers. It includes exploration of the various temperamental styles and ways to create nurturing relationships between care teachers and infants and toddlers.

Module II addresses the environmental qualities needed for the care of infants and toddlers including health, safety, comfort, convenience, child size, flexibility, movement, and choice. It also addresses the development of group-care policies based on relationships; the carrying out of the caregiving routines of feeding, diapering, and napping in a culturally responsive manner; the fostering of close relationships and learning through responsive, individualized care; and primary caregiving and continuity of care.

Module III addresses cognitive development and learning, brain development, language development and communication, and the inclusion of infants and toddlers with special needs.

Module IV addresses culture and identity formation, parent-provider relations, an approach to understanding and negotiating differences in child-rearing practices, and culturally responsive infant/toddler care. It also addresses home visitation.

References for Training Infant/Toddler Teachers from Harvard University's Center on the Developing Child

For a deeper understanding of the development of self, intentional control, and executive function, the following papers from the Center on the Developing Child at Harvard University are recommended.

National Scientific Council on the Developing Child. (2004). *Young children develop in an environment of relationships* (Working paper no. 1). Cambridge, MA: Center on the Developing Child, Harvard University.

National Scientific Council on the Developing Child. (2004). *Children's emotional development is built into the architecture of their brains* (Working paper no. 2). Cambridge, MA: Center on the Developing Child, Harvard University.

National Scientific Council on the Developing Child. (2007). *The timing and quality of early experiences combine to shape brain architecture* (Working paper no. 5). Cambridge, MA: Center on the Developing Child, Harvard University.

National Scientific Council on the Developing Child. (2010). *Early experiences can alter gene expression and affect long-term development* (Working paper no. 10). Cambridge, MA: Center on the Developing Child, Harvard University.

National Scientific Council on the Developing Child. (2011). *Building the brain's "Air Traffic Control": How early experiences shape the development of executive function* (Working paper no. 11). Cambridge, MA: Center on the Developing Child, Harvard University.

Recommended Readings

Major Studies by Economists on | the Impact of Early Investments in Children

Bartik, T. J. (2009). *Investing in kids: Early childhood programs and local economic development*. Kalamazoo, MI: W. E. Upjohn Institute for Employment Research.

Bay Area Council. (2009). *Key to economic success in the 21st century*. Retrieved from http://www.ece.marinschools.org

Britto, P. R., Yoshikawa, H., & Boller, K. (2011). Quality of early childhood development programs in global contexts—rationale for investment, conceptual framework and implications for equity. *Social Policy Report, 25*, 1–28.

Doyle, O., Harmon, C. P., Heckman, J. J., & Tremblay, R. E. (2009). Investing in early human development: Timing and economic efficiency. *Economics of Human Biology, 7*, 1–6.

Grunewald, R., & Rolnick, A. (2007). A productive investment: Early child development. In M. E. Young (Ed.), *Early child development, from measurement to action: A priority for growth and equity* (pp. 17–32). Washington, DC: The World Bank.

Heckman, J. J. (2006). Skill formation and the economics of investing in disadvantaged children. *Science, 312*, 1900–1902.

Heckman, J. J. (2007). The productivity argument for investing in young children. *Review of Agricultural Economics, 29*, 446.

Heckman, J. (2008). *Schools, skills, and synapses*. Heckman-The Economics of Human Potential. Retrieved from http://www.heckmanequation.org/content/resource/schools-skills-synapses

Knudsen, E. I., Heckman, J. J., Cameron, J. L., & Shonkoff, J. P. (2006). Economic, neurobiological, and behavioral perspectives on building America's future workforce. *Proceedings of the National Academy of Sciences of the United States of America, 103*, 10155–10162.

Lynch, R. G. (2005). *Early childhood investment yields big payoff*. Policy Perspectives. San Francisco: WestEd.

Lynch, R. G. (2007). *Enriching children, enriching the nation: Public investment in high-quality prekindergarten.* Washington, DC: Economic Policy Institute.

Rolnick, A., & Grunewald, R. (2003). *Early childhood development: Economic development with a high public return.* Federal Reserve Bank of Minneapolis. Retrieved from http://www.minneapolisfed.org/publications_papers/pub_display.cfm?id=3832

Rolnick, A., & Grunewald, R. (2007). *Early intervention at a large scale.* Minneapolis Federal Reserve Bank. Retrieved from http://www.minneapolisfed.org/research/studies/earlychild/early_intervention.cfm

References

Adetunji, Y., Macklin, D., Patel, R., & Kinsinger, L. (2003). Childhood immunizations: American College of Preventative Medicine practice policy statement. *American Journal of Preventive Medicine, 25*(2), 169–175.

American Academy of Pediatrics. (1997). Noise: A hazard for the fetus and newborn (Policy Statement). *Pediatrics, 100.* Retrieved from http://www.aap.org. policy/re9728.htm

American Academy of Pediatrics. (2000). Committee on substance abuse and committee on children with disabilities: Fetal alcohol syndrome and alcohol-related neurodevelopmental disorders. *Pediatrics, 106,* 358–361.

American Academy of Pediatrics. (2008). *Bright futures: Guidelines for health supervision of infants, children, and adolescents* (3rd ed.). Elk Grove Village, IL: American Academy of Pediatrics.

American Academy of Pediatrics. (2012). Breastfeeding and the use of human milk. *Pediatrics, 129*(3), 827–841.

Andersen, R. M. (1968). Behavioral model of families' use of health services (Research series no. 25). Chicago: Center for Health Services Administration, University of Chicago.

Andersen, R. M. (1995). Revisiting the behavioral model and access to medical care: Does it matter? *Journal of Health and Social Behavior, 36,* 1–10.

Anderson, J. E., Ebrahim, S., Floyd, L., & Atrash, H. (2006). Prevalence of risk factors for adverse pregnancy outcomes during pregnancy and the preconception period—United States, 2002–2004. *Maternal and Child Health Journal, 10,* S101–106.

Appelbaum, E., & Milkman, R. (2011). *Paid family leave pays off in California.* Retrieved from http://blogs.hbr.org/research/2011/01/paid-family-leave-pays-off-in.html

Atrash, H. K. (2005, November 29). *Preconception care: Missed opportunities to improve pregnancy outcomes.* Presentation to the Secretary's Advisory Committee on Infant Mortality, Washington, DC.

Atrash, H. K., Johnson, K., Adams, M., Cordero, J. F., & Howse, J. (2006). Preconception care for improving perinatal outcomes: The time to act. *Maternal and Child Health Journal, 10,* S3–11.

Aubrun, A., & Grady, J. (2002). *Promoting school readiness and early child development: Findings from cognitive elicitations.* Washington, DC: FrameWorks Institute.

Ball, T. M., & Wright, A. L. (1999). Health care costs of formula-feeding in the first year of life. *Pediatrics, 103*(4), 870–876.

Barker, D. J. (1995). Fetal origins of coronary heart disease. *British Medical Journal, 311,* 171–174.

Barnett, W. S. (2003). Better teachers, better preschools: Student achievement linked to teacher qualifications, *Preschool Policy Matters, 2,* 1–11. New Brunswick, NJ: National Institute for Early Education Research (NIEER), Rutgers University.

Barry, R. A., & Kochanska, G. (2010). A longitudinal investigation of the affective environment in families with young children: From infancy to early school age. *Emotion, 10*(2), 237–249.

Bartick, M., & Reinhold, A. (2010). The burden of suboptimal breastfeeding in the United States: A pediatric cost analysis. *Pediatrics, 125*(5), 1048–1056.

Bartik, T. J. (2006). *The economic development benefits of universal preschool education compared to traditional economic development programs.* Kalamazoo, MI: Committee for Economic Development.

Bartik, T. J. (2011). *Invest in kids: Early childhood programs and local economic development.* Kalamazoo, MI: W. E. Upjohn Institute for Employment Research.

Behrman, R. E. (2001). *Caring for infants and toddlers.* Los Altos, CA: David and Lucile Packard Foundation.

Belsky, J., & Fearon, R. M. P. (2008). Precursors of attachment security. In J. Cassidy and P. R. Shaver (Eds.), *Handbook of attachment theory and research* (2nd ed., pp. 295–316). New York: Guilford Press.

Bergman, K., Sarkar, P., O'Connor, T. G., Modi, N., & Glover, V. (2007). Maternal stress during pregnancy predicts cognitive ability and fearfulness in infancy. *Journal of American Academy of Child & Adolescent Psychiatry, 46,* 1454–1463.

Bernstein, P. S., Sanghvi, T., & Merkatz, I. R. (2000). Improving preconception care. *Journal of Reproductive Medicine, 45,* 546–552.

Bierman, K. L., Nix, R. L., Greenberg, M. T., Blair, C., & Domitrovich, C. E. (2008). Executive functions and school readiness intervention: Impact, moderation, and mediation in the Head Start REDI program. *Development and Psychopathology, 20,* 821–843.

Blair, C. (2002). School readiness: Integrating cognition and emotion in a neurobiological conceptualization of child functioning at school entry. *American Psychologist, 57,* 111–127.

Blair, C., Zelazo, P. D., & Greenberg, M. T. (2005). The measurement of executive function in early childhood. *Developmental Neuropsychology, 28,* 561–571.

Bloch, M., Rotenberg, N., Koren, D., & Klein, E. (2006). Risk factors for early postpartum depressive symptoms. *General Hospital Psychiatry, 28,* 3.

Bornstein, D. (2012). *The power of nursing.* Retrieved from http://opinionator. blogs.nytimes.com/2012/05/16/the-power-of-nursing/

Botto, L. D., Lisi, A., Robert-Gnansia, E., Erickson, J. D., Vollset, S. E., Mastroia-covo, P., . . . Goujard, J. (2005). International retrospective cohort study of neural tube defects in relation to folic acid recommendations: Are the recommendations working? *British Medical Journal, 330,* 571–576.

Boulet, S., Parker, C., & Atrash, H. (2006). Preconception care in international settings. *Journal of Maternal and Child Health, 10,* S29–S36.

Bowlby, J. (1982). *Attachment and loss: Vol. 1. Attachment.* New York: Basic Books. (Originally published in 1969)

Bowlby, J. (1985). The role of childhood experience in cognitive disturbance. In M. J. Mahoney and A. Freeman (Eds.), *Cognition and psychotherapy* (pp. 181–200). New York: Plenum.

Bowman, B., Donovan, S. M., & Burns, M. S. (2000). *Eager to learn: Educating our preschoolers.* Washington, DC: National Academies Press.

Brazelton, T. B. (1992). *Touchpoints: The essential reference—your child's emotional behavioral development.* Reading, MA: Perseus Books.

Brownell, C. A., & Kopp, C. B. (2007) Transitions in toddler socioemotional development: Behavior, understanding, relationships. In C. A. Brownell & C. B. Kopp (Eds.), *Socioemotional development in the toddler years* (pp. 66–69). New York: Guilford Press.

Brownell, C. A., Ramani, G. B., & Zerwas, S. (2006). Becoming a social partner with peers: Cooperation and social understanding in one- and two-year olds. *Child Development, 77,* 803–821.

Bruer, J. T. (1997). Education and the brain: A bridge too far. *Educational Researcher, 26,* 4–16.

California Child Care and Referral Network. (2006). *California early care and education workforce study: Licensed child care centers and family child care providers, 2006 statewide highlights.* Berkeley: Center for the Study of Child Care Employment, Institute of Industrial Relations, University of California.

California Department of Education. (2006). *Infant/toddler learning & development program guidelines.* Sacramento, CA: California Department of Education Press.

Calkins, S. D., & Hill, A. (2007). Caregiver influences on emerging emotion regulation: Biological and environmental transactions in early development. In J. J. Gross (Ed.), *Handbook of emotion regulation* (pp. 229–248). New York: Guilford Press.

Campbell, F. A., Pungello, E. P., Miller-Johnson, S., Burchinal, M., & Ramey, C. T. (2001). The development of cognitive and academic abilities: Growth curves from an early childhood educational experiment. *Developmental Psychology, 37*(2), 231–242.

Campbell, F. A., Ramey, C. T., Pungello, E., Sparling, J., & Miller-Johnson, S. (2002). Early childhood education: Young adult outcomes from the Abecedarian Project. *Applied Developmental Science, 6*(1), 42–57.

Carnegie Corporation of New York. (1994). *Starting points: Meeting the needs of our youngest children.* New York: Author.

Casey, P. H., & Whitt, J. K. (1980). Effect of the pediatrician on the mother-infant relationship. *Pediatrics, 65*(4), 815–820.

Caspi, A., & Shiner, R. L. (2006). Personality development. In W. Damon & R. Lerner (Series Eds.) & N. Eisenberg (Vol. Ed.), *Handbook of child psychology* (Vol. 3): Social, emotional, and personality development (6th ed., pp. 300–365). New York: Wiley.

Cefalo, R. C., & Moos, M. K. (1995). *Preconceptional health care: A practical guide.* St. Louis, MO: Mosby.

Centers for Disease Control and Prevention. (2006). *Preconception care and health.* Retrieved from http://www.cdc.gov/ncbddd/preconception/documents/At-a-glance-4-11-06.pdf

Centers for Disease Control and Prevention. (2011a). *Breastfeeding report card: United States, 2011.* Atlanta: Department of Health and Human Services.

Centers for Disease Control and Prevention. (2011b). *The CDC guide to breastfeeding interventions: Maternity care practices.* Retrieved from http://www.cdc.gov/breastfeeding/pdf/BF_guide_1.pdf

Centers for Disease Control and Prevention. (2012a). *Birth data.* Retrieved from http://www.cdc.gov/nchs/births.htm

Centers for Disease Control and Prevention. (2012b). *Unintended pregnancy prevention.* Retrieved from http://www.cdc.gov/reproductivehealth/unintendedpregnancy/

Chatterji, P., & Markowitz, S. (2008). *Family leave after childbirth and the health of new mothers.* Cambridge, MA: National Bureau of Economic Research.

Child Trends. (2010). *Toward the identification of features of effective professional development for early childhood educators.* Washington, DC: U.S. Department of Education Office of Planning, Evaluation, and Policy Development Policy and Program Studies Service.

Chung, M., Raman, G., Trikalinos, T., Lau, J., & Ip, S. (2008). Interventions in primary care to promote breastfeeding: An evidence review for the U.S. Preventive Services Task Force. *Annals of Internal Medicine, 149,* 565–582.

Cody, J. (2009). *Home pregnancy tests can lead to better prenatal care.* Retrieved from http://www.medicalnewstoday.com/releases/138666.php

Cohen, L. S., & Nonacs, R. M. (Eds.). (2005). Mood and anxiety disorders during pregnancy and postpartum. Washington, DC: American Psychiatric Publishing.

Coles, C. (1994). Critical periods for prenatal alcohol exposure: Evidence from animal and human studies. *Alcohol Health and Research World, 18,* 22–29.

Consortium on the School-based Promotion of Social Competence. (1994). The school-based promotion of social competence: Theory, research, practice, and policy. In R. J. Haggerty, L. R. Sherrod, N. Garmezy, & M. Rutter (Eds.), *Stress, risk, and resilience in children and adolescents: Processes, mechanisms, and interventions* (pp. 268–316). Cambridge, UK: Cambridge University Press.

Cooper, P., Murray, L., & Stein, A. (1993). Psychosocial factors associated with the early termination of breastfeeding. *Journal of Psychosomatic Research, 37,* 171–176.

Council on Pediatric Practice. (1967). *Standards of child health care.* Evanston, IL: American Academy of Pediatrics.

Cragan, J. D., Friedman, J. M., Holmes, L. B., Uhl, K., Green, N. S., & Riley, L. (2006). Ensuring the safe and effective use of medications during pregnancy: Planning and prevention through preconception care. *Maternal and Child Health Journal, 10,* S129–135.

Culhane, J., Elo, F., Irma, T. (2005). Neighbourhood context and reproductive health. *American Journal of Obstetrics and Gynecology, 192*(Supplement 1), S22–S29.

Cunha, F., & Heckman, J. (2007). *The technology of skill formation* (NBER working paper no. 12840). Retrieved from http://www.nber.org/papers/w12840. pdf?new_window=1

Cutler, D. (2010). How health care reform must bend the cost curve. *Health Affairs, 29*(6), 1131–1135.

Dacey, J. S., & Travers, J. F. (2002). *Human development across the lifespan.* New York: McGraw-Hill.

Datta Gupta, N., Smith, N., & Verner, M. (2008). Perspective article: The impact of Nordic countries' family friendly policies on employment, wages, and children. *Review of Economics of the Household, 6,* 65–89.

Dawson, G., Ashman, S., & Carver, L. (2000). The role of early experience in shaping behavioral and brain development and its implications for social policy. *Development and Psychopathology, 12,* 695–712.

DeCasper, A. J., & Fifer, W. P. (1980). Of human bonding: Newborns prefer their mothers' voices. *Science, 208*(4448), 1174–1176.

Delissaint, D., & McKyer, E. L. (2011). A systematic review of factors utilized in preconception health behavior research. *Health Education and Behavior, 28,* 603–615.

Delvoye, P., Guillaume, C., Collard, S., Nardella, T., & Mauroy, M. (2008, August 28). *Preconception health promotion means and constraints analysis.* Presentation at the 1st Central and Eastern European Summit on Preconception Health and Prevention of Birth Defects, Budapest, Hungary.

Denham, S. A. (1998). *Emotional development in young children.* New York: Guilford Press.

Denham, S. A. (2006). Social-emotional competence as support for school readiness: What is it and how do we assess it? *Early Education and Development, 17,* 57–89.

Department of Labor Bureau of Statistics. (2006). *National compensation survey.* Retrieved http://www.bls.gov/ncs/ebs/sp/ebsm0004.pdf

Diamond, A. (2010). The evidence base for improving school outcomes by addressing the whole child and by addressing skills and attitudes, not just content. *Early Education and Development, 21,* 780–793.

Dietz, P., Williams, S., Callagham, W., Bachman, D. J.,Whitlock, E. P., & Hornbrook, M. C. (2007). Clinically identified maternal depression before, during, and after pregnancies ending in live births. *American Journal of Psychiatry, 164*, 1515.

Drury, S., Theall, K. P., Smyke, A. T., Keats, B. J. B., Egger, H. L., Nelson, C. A., . . . Zeanah, C. H. (2010). Modification of depression by COMT val158met polymorphism in children exposed to early severe psychosocial deprivation. *Child Abuse and Neglect, 34*, 387–395.

Dyson, L., McCormick, F. M., & Renfrew, M. J. (2005). Interventions for promoting the initiation of breastfeeding. *Cochrane Database of Systematic Reviews, 18*(2), CD001688.

Ebrahim, S., Lo, S., Zhuo, J., Han, J.-Y., Delvoye, P., & Zhu, L. (2006). Models of preconception care implementation in selected countries. *Journal of Maternal and Child Health, 10*(Suppl. 1), 37–42.

Eisenberg, N. (2000). Emotion, regulation, and moral development. *Annual Review of Psychology, 51*, 665–697.

Eisenberg, N., Hofer, C., & Vaughan, J. (2007). Effortful control and its socioemotional consequences. In J. J. Gross (Ed.), *Handbook of emotion regulation*. New York: Guilford Press.

Evans, J., Heron, J., Francomb, H., Oke, S., & Golding, J. (2001). Cohort study of depressed mood during pregnancy and after childbirth. *British Medical Journal, 323*(7307), 257–260.

Every Child by Two. (2012). *Childhood vaccines save lives and money*. Retrieved from http://www.ecbt.org/advocates

Falceto, O. G., Giugliani, E. R., & Fernandes, C. L. (2004). Influence of parental mental health on early termination of breast-feeding: A case-control study. *Journal of the American Board and Family Practice, 17*(3), 173–183.

Families and Work Institute. (1996). *Rethinking the brain: New insights into early development. Conference report—Brain development in young children: New frontiers for research, policy and practice*. New York: Author.

Feldman, P. J., Dunkel-Schetter, C., Sandman, C. A., & Wadhwa, P. D. (2000). Maternal social support predicts birth weight and fetal growth in human pregnancy. *Psychosomatic Medicine, 62*, 15.

Field, T. (1992). Infants of depressed mothers. *Developmental Psychology, 4*, 49–66.

Field, T. (1998). Maternal depression: Effects on infants and early interventions. *Preventive Medicine, 27*, 200–203.

Finer, L. B., & Henshaw, S. K. (2006). Disparities in rates of unintended pregnancy in the United States, 1994 and 2001. *Perspectives on Sexual and Reproductive Health, 38(2)*, 90–96.

Fleming, M. F., Mundt, M. P., French, M. T., Manwell, L. B., Stauffacher, E. A., & Barry, K. L. (2002). Brief physician advice for problem alcohol drinkers: Long-term efficacy and benefit-cost analysis. *Alcoholism, Clinical, and Experimental Research, 26*(2), 36–43.

Forman, D., Videbech, P., Hedegaard, M., Dalby, J., & Secher, N. J. (2000). Post-partum depression: Identification of women at risk. *BJOG: an International Journal of Obstetrics and Gynaecology, 107*(10), 1210–1217.

Fox, N. A., & Calkins, S. D. (2003). The development of self control of emotion: Intrinsic and extrinsic influences. *Motivation and Emotion, 27*(1), 7–26.

Frank Porter Graham Child Development Institute. (2012). *The Abecedarian project.* Retrieved from http://projects.fpg.unc.edu/~abc/

Fuller, B., Kagan, S., Loeb, S., & Chang, Y. (2004). Child care quality: Centers and home settings that serve poor families. *Early Childhood Research Quarterly, 19,* 505–527.

Galler, J. R., Harrison, R. H., Biggs, M. A., Ramsey, F., & Forde, V. (1999). Maternal moods predict breastfeeding in Barbados. *Journal of Developmental and Behavioral Pediatrics, 20*(2), 80–87.

Gallese, N. (2001). The "shared manifold" hypothesis—From mirror neurons to empathy. *Journal of Consciousness Studies, 8,* 33–50.

Gentilello, L. M., Ebel, B. E., Wickizer, T. M., Salkever, D. S., & Rivara, F. P. (2005). Alcohol interventions for trauma patients treated in emergency departments and hospitals: A cost benefit analysis. *Annals of Surgery, 241*(4), 541–550.

Gerber, M. (2012). *Magda Gerber quotes: Seeing babies with new eyes.* Retrieved from http://www.magdagerber.org/3/post/2012/04/magda-quotes.html

Gestation Diabetes in France Study Group. (1991). Multicenter survey of diabetic pregnancy in France. *Diabetes Care, 14(11),* 994–1000.

Goldman, D. P., & Lakdawalla, D. N. (2010, December). Can the ACA improve population health? *The Economists' Voice,* 1–5.

Gomby, D., & Pei, D. J. (2009). *Newborn family leave: Effects on children, parents, and business.* Los Altos, CA: David and Lucile Packard Foundation.

Gornick, J. C., & Meyers, M. K. (2003). *Families that work: Policies for reconciling parenthood and employment.* New York: Russell Sage Foundation.

Greenspan, S. I. (1990). Emotional development in infants and toddlers. In J. R. Lally (Ed.), *Infant/toddler caregiving: A guide to social-emotional growth and socialization* (pp. 15–18). Sacramento: California Department of Education.

Grjibovski, A., Bygren, L. O., Svartbo, B., & Magnus, P. (2004). Housing conditions, perceived stress, smoking, and alcohol: Determinants of fetal growth in Northwest Russia. *Acta obstetricia et gynecologica Scandinavica, 83,* 1159.

Grosse, S. D. (2004). Does newborn screening save money? The difference between cost-effective and cost-saving interventions. *Journal of Pediatrics, 146*(2), 168–170.

Grosse, S. D., Sotnikkov, S. V., Leatherman, S., & Curtis, M. (2006). The business case for preconception care: Methods and issues. *Maternal Child Health Journal, 10*(5[Suppl. 5]), 93–99.

Grossmann, K., Grossmann, K. E., Kindler, H., & Zimmermann, P. (2008) A wider view of attachment and exploration: The influence of mothers and fathers on the development of psychological security from infancy to young adulthood. In J. Cassidy & P. R. Shaver (Eds.), *Handbook of attachment: Theory, research, and clinical applications.* (2nd ed., pp. 857–879). New York: Guilford Press.

Hakim, R. B., & Ronsaville, D. S. (2002). Effect of compliance with health supervision guidelines among U.S. infants on emergency department visits. *Archives of Pediatrics & Adolescent Medicine, 156*(10), 1015–1020.

Halberstadt, A. G., Denham, S. A., & Dunsmore, J. C. (2001). Affective social competence. *Social Development, 10,* 79–119.

Halbreich, U. (2005). Postpartum disorders: Multiple interacting underlying mechanisms and risk factors. *Journal of Affective Disorders, 88,* 1.

Hamburg, D. A. (1995). *President's essay: A developmental strategy to prevent lifelong damage.* Retrieved from http://carnegie.org/fileadmin/Media/Publications/PDF/A Developmental Strategy to Prevent Lifelong Damage.pdf

Han, W.-J., Ruhm, C., Waldfogel, J., & Washbrook, E. (2008). The timing of mothers' employment after childbirth. *Monthly Labor Review,* 15–27.

Han, W.-J., & Waldfogel, J. (2003). Parental leave: The impact of recent legislation on parents' leave taking. *Demography, 40*(1), 191–200.

Harms, T., & Clifford, R. (1980). *Early childhood environmental rating scale.* New York: Teachers College Press.

Harms, T., Cryer, D., & Clifford, R. (1990). *Infant/toddler environmental rating scale.* New York: Teachers College Press.

Harris, I. (1994). *Should public policy be concerned with early childhood development?* Chicago: Harris Graduate School of Public Policy Studies, University of Chicago.

Harvard Medical School. (2004). *Inside the greenhouse: The impacts of CO_2 and climate change on public health in the inner city.* Boston: Center for Health and the Global Environment.

Hatton, D. C., Harrison-Hohner, J., Coste, S., Dorato, V., Curet, L. B., & McCarron, D. A. (2005). Symptoms of postpartum depression and breastfeeding. *Journal of Human Lactation, 21,* 444–449.

Hawkins, S. S., Griffiths, L. J., Dezateux, C., Law, C., & Millennium Cohort Study Child Health Group. (2007). The impact of maternal employment on breastfeeding duration in the U.K. Millennium Cohort Study. *Public Health Nutrition, 10*(9), 891–896.

Hayghe, H. (1984, December). Working mothers reach record number in 1984. *Monthly Labor Review,* 31–34.

Heckman, J. (2000). Policies to foster human capital. *Research in Economics, 54,* 3–56.

Heckman, J. (2006a, January 10). Catch 'em young. *Wall Street Journal,* A14.

Heckman, J. (2006b). The technology and neuroscience of capacity formation. *Proceedings of the National Academy of Sciences, 104*(3), 13250–13255.

Heckman, J. (2008). Schools, skills, and synapses. *Economic Inquiry, 46,* 289–324.

Heckman, J. (2012). *The Heckman Equation.* Retrieved from http://www.heckmanequation.org/content/resource/presenting-heckman-equation

Heckman, J., & Masterov, D. (2004). *The productivity argument for investing in young children*. Chicago: Invest in Kids Working Group Committee for Economic Development.

Helburn, S. W. (1995). *Cost, quality, and child outcomes in child care centers*. Denver: Department of Economics, Center for Research in Economics and Social Policy, Univeristy of Colorado at Denver.

Henderson, J. J., Evans, S. F., & Straton, J. A., et al. (2003). Impact of postnatal depression on breastfeeding duration. *Birth, 30*, 175–180.

Henshaw, S. K. (1998). Abortion incidence and services in the United States, 1995–1996. *Family Planning Perspectives, 30*(6), 263–270, 287.

Heymann, J., Earle, A., & Hayes, J. (2007). *Work, family, and equity index: How does the United States measure up?* Cambridge, MA: Harvard University.

Hobel, C. J., Goldstein, A., & Barrett, E. S. (2008). Psychosocial stress and pregnancy outcome. *Clinical obstetrics and gynecology, 51*, 333–348.

Horwitz, S. M., Briggs-Gowan, M. J., Storfer-Isser, A., & Carter, A. S. (2009). Persistence of maternal depressive symptoms throughout the early years of childhood. *Journal of Women's Health, 18*(5), 637–645.

Howes, C. (1983). Patterns of friendship. *Child Development, 54*(4), 1041–1053.

Howes, C., Hamilton, C. E., & Matheson, C. C. (1994). Children's relationships with peers: Differential association with aspects of the teacher-child relationship. *Child Development, 65*(1), 253–263.

Howes, C., & Matheson, C. C. (1992). Sequences in the development of competent play with peers: Social and pretend play. *Developmental Psychology, 28*(5), 961–974.

Howes, C., Phillips, A., & Whitebook, M. (1992). Thresholds of quality: Implications for the social development of children in center-based child care. *Child Development, 63*, 449–460.

Hoyert, D. L., Kung, H. C., & Smith, B. L. (2005). Deaths: Preliminary data for 2003. *National Vital Statistics, 53*, 1–48.

Human Resources and Community Development Division of the Congressional Budget Office. (1983). *Demographic and social trends: Implications for federal support of dependent-care services for children and the elderly*. Washington, DC: U.S. House of Representatives.

Hykin, J., Moore, R., Duncan, K., Clare, S., Baker, S., Johnson, I., Botwell, R., Mansfield, P., & Gowland, P. (1999). Fetal brain activity demonstrated by functional magnetic resonance imaging. *The Lancet, 354*, 645–646.

Ip, S., Chung, M., Raman, G., Chew, P., Magula, N., DeVine, D., Trikalinos, T., & Lau, J. (2007). *Breastfeeding and maternal and infant health outcomes in developed countries*. Rockville, MD: Agency for Healthcare Research and Quality.

Irwin, L. G., Siddiqi, A., & Hertzman, C. (2007). Early child development: A powerful equalizer. World Health Organization's Commission on the Social Determinants of Health.

Jayson, S. (2011). Unplanned pregnancies in states reach 4 in 10. Retrieved from http://www.usatoday.com/news/health/wellness/pregnancy/story/2011/05/40-of-pregnancies-across-USA-unplanned-study-finds/47316772/1

Jennings, K., Ross, S., Popper, S., & Elmore, M. (1999). Thoughts of harming infants in depressed and nondepressed mothers. *Journal of Affective Disorders, 54*(1–2), 21–28.

Jones, L. B., Rothbart, M. K., & Posner, M. I. (2003). Development of executive attention in preschool children. *Developmental Science, 6*(5), 498–504.

Kalnins, L. V., & Bruner, J. S. (1973). The coordination of visual observation and instrumental behavior in early infancy. *Perception, 2,* 307–314.

Katz, L. (2012). *Favorite quotes: Lilian Katz and Edward Zigler, Ph.D.* Retrieved from http://talaemccray.blogspot.com/2010/11/favorite-quotes-lilian-katz-and-edward.html

Keniston, K. (1985). The myth of family independence. In J. M. Henslin (Ed.), *Marriage and family in a changing society* (pp. 27–33). New York: Free Press.

Kent, H., Johnson, K., Curtis, M., Hood, J. R., & Atrash, H. (2006). Proceedings of the preconception health and health care clinical, public health, and consumer workgroup meetings. Atlanta, GA: Centers for Disease Control and Prevention, National Center on Birth Defects and Developmental Disabilities.

Kieras, J. E., Tobin, R. M., Graziano, W. G., & Rothbart, M. K. (2005). You can't always get what you want: Effortful control and children's responses to undesirable gifts. *Psychological Science, 16*(5), 391–396.

Kinzler, K. D., Shutts, K., DeJesus, J., & Spelke, E. S. (2009). Accent trumps race in guiding children's social preferences. *Social Cognition, 27,* 623–634.

Kisilevsky, B. S., Hains, S. M., Lee, K., Xie, X., Huang, H., Ye, H. H., . . . Wang, Z. (2003). Effects of experience on fetal voice recognition. *Psychological Science, 14,* 220–224.

Kitzman, H., Olds, D. L., Sidora, K., Henderson, C. R., Hanks, C., & Cole, R., . . . Glazner, J. (2000). Enduring effects of nurse home visitation on maternal life course: A 3-year follow-up of a randomized trial. *JAMA: The Journal of the American Medical Association, 283*(15), 1983–1989.

Klaus, M. H., Kennell, J. H., & Klaus, P. H. (1995). *Bonding: Building the foundations of secure attachment and independence.* New York: Addison-Wesley.

Knudsen, E. I. (2004). Sensitive periods in the development of the brain and behavior. *Journal of Cognitive Neuroscience, 16,* 1412–1425.

Kochanska, G., Aksan, N., Knaack, A., & Rhines, H. M. (2004). Maternal parenting and children's conscience: Early security as a moderator. *Child Development, 75*(4), 1229–1242.

Kochanska, G., Koenig, J. L., Barry, R. A., Kim, S., & Yoon, J. E. (2010). Children's conscience during toddler and preschool years, moral self, and a competent, adaptive developmental trajectory. *Developmental Psychology, 46*(5), 1320–1332.

Kopp, C. B. (2003). *Baby steps* (2nd ed.). New York, NY: Henry Holt.

Kramer, M. S., & Kakuma, R. (2002). *Optimal duration of exclusive breastfeeding: A systematic review.* Geneva, Switzerland: World Health Organization.

Kuo, A. A., Inkelas, M., Lotstein, D. S., Samson, K. M., Schor, E. L., & Halfon, N. (2006). Rethinking well-child care in the United States: An international comparison. *Pediatrics, 118,* 1692–1702.

Lagattuta, K. H., & Wellman, H. M. (2002). Differences in early parent-child conversations about negative versus positive emotions: Implications for the development of psychological understanding. *Developmental Psychology, 38*(4), 564–580.

Lagoy, C. T., Joshi, N., Cragan, J. D., & Rasmussen, S. A. (2005). Medication use during pregnancy and lactation: An urgent call for public health action. *Journal of Women's Health, 14*(2), 104–109.

Laible, D. (2004). Mother-child discourse in two contexts: Links with child temperament, attachment security, and socioemotional competence. *Developmental Psychology, 40*(6), 979–992.

Lally, J. R. (2006). Metatheories of childrearing. In J. R. Lally, P. L. Mangione, & D. Greenwald (Eds.), *Concepts for care: 20 essays on infant/toddler development and learning* (pp. 7–14). San Francisco: WestEd.

Lally, J. R. (2009, November). The science and psychology of infant–toddler care. *ZERO TO THREE Journal,* 34–40.

Lally, J. R. (2010). School readiness begins in infancy. *Kappan Magazine, 922*(3), 17–21.

Lally, J. R. (2011). The link between consistent caring interactions with babies, early brain development, and school readiness. In E. Zigler, W. S. Gilliam, & W. S. Barnett (Eds.), *The pre-K debates: Current controversies and issues.* Baltimore, MD: Brookes.

Lambers, D. S., & Clarke, K. E. (1996). The maternal and fetal physiologic effects of nicotine. *Serine Perinatol, 20,* 115–126.

Landau, B., & Spelke, E. (1988). Geometric complexity and object search in infancy. *Developmental Psychology, 24,* 512–521.

Lawson, J. (2010). *Functional perspectives: The far side of despair.* Retrieved from http://www.reichian.com/despair.htm

Leach, P. (2012). *Understanding your toddler.* Retrieved from http://www.babycentre.co.uk/toddler/penelopeleach/understandingyourtoddler/

Legislation and National Strategies. (2011). *FASD prevention in France: Zero alcool pendant la grossesse.* Retrieved from http://fasdprevention.wordpress.com/2011/05/12/fasd-prevention-in-france/

Lenroot, R. K., & Giedd, J. N. (2006). Brain development in children and adolescents: Insights from anatomical magnetic resonance imaging. *Neuroscience and Biobehavioral Reviews, 30,* 718–729.

Leong, D. J. (2011, October 21). *Understanding the role of the infant care teacher in a child's development of executive function.* Presented at the Program for Infant/Toddler Care Graduate Conference, Berkeley, CA.

Lindberg, L. (1996). Women's decisions about breastfeeding and maternal employment. *Journal of Marriage and the Family, 58,* 239–251.

Loftus, M. J. (2006, Spring). What babies know. *Emory Magazine,* 13–14.

Losch, M., Dungy, C. I., Russell, D., & Dusdieker, L. B. (1995). Impact of attitudes on maternal decisions regarding infant feeding. *Journal of Pediatrics, 126*(4), 507–514.

Lovell, V., O'Neill, E., & Olsen, S. (2007). Maternity leave in the United States: Paid parental leave is still not standard, even among best U.S. employers. Washington, DC: Institute for Women's Policy Research.

Lu, M. C., Tache, G. R., Kotelchuck, M., & Halfon, N. (2003). Preventing low birth weight: Is prenatal care the answer? *Journal of Maternal-Fetal and Neonatal Medicine, 13,* 362–380.

Lynch, R. G. (2004). Exceptional returns: Economic, fiscal, and social benefits of investment in early childhood development. Washington, DC: Economic Policy Institute.

March of Dimes Birth Defects Foundation. (2004). Folic acid and the prevention of birth defects: A national survey of pre-pregnancy awareness and behavior among women of childbearing age, 1995–2004. White Plains, NY: March of Dimes.

Marks, J. S., Koplan, J. P., Hogue, C. J., & Dalmat, M. E. (1990). A cost-benefit/cost-effectiveness analysis of smoking cessation for pregnant women. *American Journal of Preventive Medicine, 6*(5), 282–289.

Marvin, R. S., & Britner, P. A. (2008). Normative development: The ontogeny of attachment. In J. Cassidy and P. R. Shaver (Eds.), *Handbook of attachment theory and research* (2nd ed.). New York: Guilford Press.

Masse, L. N., & Barnett, W. S. (2002). *A benefit cost analysis of the Abecedarian early childhood intervention.* New Brunswick, NJ: National Institute for Early Education Research.

McEwen, B. S. (1998). Protective and damaging effects of stress mediators. *New England Journal of Medicine, 338,* 171–179.

McQuiston, S., & Kloczko, N. (2011). Speech and language development: Monitoring process and problems. *Pediatrics, 23,* 230–239.

Meaney, M. J. (2001). Maternal care, gene expression, and the transmission of individual differences in stress reactivity across generations. *Annual Review of Neuroscience, 24,* 1161–1192.

Meara, E., Kotagal, U. R., Atherton, H. D., & Lieu, T. A. (2004). Impact on early newborn discharge legislation and early follow-up visits on infant outcomes in a state Medicaid population. *Pediatrics, 113*(6), 1619–1627.

Minnesota Center for Health Statistics. (2010). *Family home visiting background information.* Retrieved from http://www.health.state.mn.us/divs/chs/

Minnesota Department of Health. (2009). *2009 Minnesota county health tables.* Retrieved from http://www.health.state.mn.us/divs/chs/countytables/profiles2009/index.html

Moore, K. L. (1988). The urogenital system. In K. L. Moore (Ed.), *The developing human* (pp. 246–326). Philadelphia: Saunders.

Mustin, H. D., Holt, V. L., & Connell, F. A. (1994). Adequacy of well-child care and immunizations in U.S. infants born in 1988. *JAMA: The Journal of the American Medical Association, 272,* 1111–1115.

Nagy, E. (2011). The newborn infant: A missing stage in developmental psychology. *Infant and Child Development, 20,* 3–19.

National Association of Child Care Resource and Referral Agencies. (2006). *We can do better: NACCRRA's ranking of state child care center regulation and oversight.* Arlington, VA: Author.

National Association of Child Care Resource and Referral Agencies. (2011). *We can do better: NACCRRA's ranking of state child care center regulations and oversight.* Arlington, VA: Author.

National Business Group on Health. (2007). *Investing in maternal and child health: A business imperative.* Washington, DC: Author.

National Campaign to Prevent Teen and Unplanned Pregnancy. (2012). *Unplanned pregnancy in the United States among all women.* Retrieved from http://www.thenationalcampaign.org/resources/dcr/SectionA/DCR_SectionA.pdf

National Development and Research Institutes. (2012). *Infection during pre/post-pregnancy stage like influenza, pneumonia, sexually transmitted disease (STD) have stronger effect on babies health even leukemia.* Retrieved from http://ndri.com/news/infection_during_pre__postpregnancy_stage_like_influenza_pneumonia_sexually_transmitted_disease_std.html

National Institutes of Health. (2010). *Health economics: NIH research priorities for health care reforms* (Meeting summary). Bethesda, MD: Author.

National Institute of Child Health and Human Development (NICHD). (2006). *NICHD study of early child care and youth development.* Washington, DC: U.S. Department of Health and Human Services.

NICHD Early Child Care Research Network. (2000). Characteristics and quality of child care for toddlers and preschoolers. *Applied Developmental Science, 4*(3), 116–135.

National Scientific Council on the Developing Child. (2007a). *The science of early childhood development: Closing the gap between what we know and what we do.* Cambridge, MA: Center on the Developing Child, Harvard University.

National Scientific Council on the Developing Child. (2007b). *The timing and quality of early experiences combine to shape brain architecture.* Cambridge, MA: Center on the Developing Child, Harvard University.

National Scientific Council on the Developing Child. (2008). *Mental health problems in early childhood can impair learning and behavior for life* (Working paper no. 6). Retrieved from http://developingchild.harvard.edu/

National Scientific Council on the Developing Child. (2010). *Early experiences can alter gene expression and affect long-term development.* Cambridge, MA: Center on the Developing Child, Harvard University.

National Scientific Council on the Developing Child. (2011). *Building the brain's "air traffic control" system: How early experiences shape the development of executive function.* Cambridge, MA: Center on the Developing Child, Harvard University.

National Scientific Council on the Developing Child. (2012). *Foundations of lifelong health.* Retrieved from http://developingchild.harvard.edu/topics/ foundations_of_lifelong_health/

National Women's Health Resource Center. (2007). *Breastfeeding at work: Toughest for younger moms and retail workers.* Retrieved from http://www. healthywomen.org/content/press-release/breastfeeding-work-toughest-younger-moms-and-retail-workers

Nelson, C. (2007). The neurobiological perspective on early human deprivation. *Child Development Perspectives, 1,* 13–18.

Norbeck, J., & Tilden, V. (1983). Life stress, social support, and emotional disequilibrium in complications of pregnancy: A prospective, multivariate study. *Journal of Health and Social Behavior, 24,* 30–46.

Oddy, W., Sly, P., de Klerk, N., Landau, L., Kendall, G., Holt, P., Stanley, F. (2003). Breastfeeding and respiratory morbidity in infancy: A birth cohort study. *Archives of Disease in Childhood, 88*(3), 224–228.

Office of Health Statistics and Assessment. (2010). *Prevention pays.* Tallahassee, FL: Florida Department of Health.

Olds, D., Henderson, C., Phelps, C., Kitzman, H., & Hanks, C. (1993). Effect of prenatal and infancy nurse home visitation on government spending. *Medical Care, 31*(2), 155–174.

Oppenheim, D., Sagi, A., & Lamb, M. E. (1988). Infant-adult attachments on the kibbutz and their relation to socioemotional development 4 years later. *Developmental Psychology, 24*(3), 427–433.

Pawl, J. (2006). Being held in another's mind. In J. R. Lally, P. L. Mangione, & D. Greenwald (Eds.), *Concepts for care.* San Francisco: WestEd.

Pawl, J. (2011). *Oklahoma Association for Infant Mental Health.* Retrieved from http://www.okaimh.org/uploads/Endorsement_Fly_Feb_2012.pdf

Pawl, J. H., & John, M. S. (1995). *How you are is as important as what you do.* Washington, DC: ZERO TO THREE.

Pew Research Center. (2009). *The harried life of the working mother.* Washington, DC: Author.

Pinker, S. (2003). The blank slate: The modern denial of human nature. London: Penguin Group.

Piper, S., & Parks, P. L. (1996). Predicting the duration of lactation: Evidence from a national survey. *Birth, 23,* 7–12.

Pritchard, C. W., & Teo, P. Y. (1994). Preterm birth, low birthweight and the stressfulness of the household role for pregnant women. *Social Science Medicine, 38,* 89–96.

Quann, V., & Wien, C. (2006). The visible empathy of infants and toddlers. *Young Children, 61*(4), 23–29.

Reece, E. A., Leguizamon, G., Silva, J., Whiteman, V., & Smith, D. (2002). Intensive interventional maternity care reduces infant morbidity and hospital costs. *Journal of Maternal-Fetal & Neonatal Medicine, 11*(3), 204–210.

Reeve, M. (2009). Preconception health: The missing link in the MNCH continuum of care. *Journal of Peking University Health Sciences, 41*(4), 383–388.

Reynolds, A. J., Temple, J. A., Ou, S., Arteaga, I. A., & White, B. (2011). School-based early childhood education and age-28 well-being: Effects by timing, dosage, and subgroups. *Science, 333*(6040), 360–364.

Rochat, P. (2004). *The infant's world.* Cambridge, MA: Harvard University Press.

Rochman, B. (2012). *Why most moms don't reach their own breast-feeding goals.* Retrieved from http://healthland.time.com/2012/06/04/why-most-moms-cant-reach-their-own-breast-feeding-goals/#ixzz20vDLhSFI

Rogers, B. P., Morgan, V. L., Newton, A. T., & Gore, J. C. (2007). Assessing functional connectivity in the human brain by fMRI. *Magnetic Resonance Imaging, 10,* 1347–1357.

Rolnick, A., & Grunewald, R. (2003). *Early childhood development: Economic development with a high public return.* Minneapolis, MN: Federal Reserve Bank of Minneapolis.

Ross, M. G., Sandhu, M., Bemis, R., Nessim, S., Bragonier, J. R., & Hobel, C. (1994). The West Los Angeles Preterm Birth Prevention Project: II. Cost-effectiveness analysis of high-risk pregnancy interventions. *Obstetrics and Gynecology, 83*(4), 504–511.

Ruhm, C. (2000). Parental leave and child health. *Journal of Health Economics, 19*(6), 931–960.

Rutledge, J. C. (1997). Developmental toxicity induced during early stages of mammalian embryogenesis. *Mutation Research, 396,* 113–127.

Saarni, C., Campos, J. J., Camras, L., & Witherington, D. (2006). Emotional development: Action, communication, and understanding. In W. Damon, R. Lerner, & N. Eisenberg (Eds.), *Handbook of child psychology* (Vol. 3). New York: Wiley.

Santrock, J. W. (1995). *Life-span development.* Madison, WI: Brown & Benchmark.

Santrock, J. W. (2006). *Life-span development.* New York: McGraw-Hill.

Schore, A. (2000). Attachment and the regulation of the right brain. *Attachment and Human Development, 2,* 23–47.

Schore, A. (2001a). Contributions from the decade of the brain to infant mental health: An overview. *Infant Mental Health Journal, 22,* 1–2.

Schore, A. (2001b). The effects of a secure attachment relationship on right brain development, affect regulation, and infant mental health. *Infant Mental Health Journal, 22,* 7–66.

Schore, A. (2003). *Affect dysregulation and disorders of the self.* New York: W. W. Norton.

Schore, A. (2005). Attachment, affect regulation, and the developing right brain: Linking developmental neuroscience to pediatrics. *Pediatrics in Review, 26,* 204–217.

Sebelius, K. (2011). *Race to the Top—Early learning challenge.* Retrieved from http://www.hhs.gov/secretary/about/speeches/sp20110524.html

Seidman, D. (1998). Postpartum psychiatric illness: The role of the pediatrician. *Pediatrics in Review, 19*(4), 128–131.

Shonkoff, J. P., & Phillips, D. (Eds.). (2000). *From neurons to neighborhoods.* Washington, DC: National Academies Press.

Shore, R. (1997). *Rethinking the brain: New insights into early development.* New York: Families and Work Institute.

Siega-Riz, A. M., & Laraia, B. (2006). The implications of maternal overweight and obesity on the course of pregnancy and birth outcomes. *Maternal Child Health Journal, 10*(5 Suppl.), S153–S156.

Siegel, D. J. (1999). *The developing mind.* New York: Guilford Press.

Siegler, R. S., DeLoache, J. S., & Eisenberg, N. (2006). *How children develop* (2nd ed., with supplemental media toolkit). New York: Worth.

Smith, K., Downs, B., & O'Connell, M. (2011). *Maternity leave and employment patterns: 1961–1995.* Washington, DC: U.S. Census Bureau.

Snow, K. L. (2006). Measuring school readiness: Conceptual and practical considerations. *Early Education and Development, 17,* 7–41.

Spence, S., Shapiro, D., & Zaidel, E. (1996). The role of the right hemisphere in the physiological and cognitive components of emotional processing. *Psychophysiology, 33,* 112–122.

Sroufe, L. A. (1996). *Emotional development.* Cambridge, UK: Cambridge University Press.

Stuebe, A. (2009). The risks of not breastfeeding for mothers and infants. *Reviews in Obstetrics and Gynecology, 2*(4), 222–231.

Tanaka, S. (2005). Parental leave and child health across OECD countries. *Economic Journal, 115,* F7–28.

Task Force on Community Preventive Services. (2003). First reports evaluating the effectiveness of strategies for preventing violence: Early childhood home visitation. Atlanta: Centers for Disease Control and Prevention.

Taumoepeau, M., & Ruffman, T. (2008). Stepping stones to others' minds: Maternal talk relates to child mental state language and emotion understanding at 15, 24, and 33 months. *Child Development, 79*(2), 284–302.

Tavares, J. V., Drevets, W. C., & Sahakian, B. (2003). Cognition in mania and depression. *Psychological Medicine, 33,* 959–967.

Thompson, R. A. (2009). Doing what doesn't come naturally. *ZERO TO THREE Journal, 30,* 33–39.

Thompson, R. A. (2010). *Connecting neurons, concepts, and people: Brain development and its implications.* New Brunswick, NJ: National Institute for Early Education Research, Rutgers Graduate School of Education.

Thompson, R. A. (2011). The emotionate child. In D. Cicchetti & G. I. Roisman (Eds.), *Minnesota symposium on child psychology: The origins and organization of adaptation and maladaptation.* Hoboken, NJ: Wiley.

Thompson, R. A., & Meyer, S. (2007). Socialization of emotion regulation in the family. In J. J. Gross (Ed.), *Handbook of emotion regulation*. New York: Guilford Press.

Thompson, R. A., & Nelson, C. A. (2001). Developmental science and the media: Early brain development. *American Psychologist, 56*(1), 5–15.

Thompson, R. A., Thompson, J. E., & Luckenbill, J. (2011). The developing brain and its importance to relationships, temperament, and self-regulation. In J. R. Lally (Ed.), *A guide to social-emotional growth and socialization* (2nd ed.). Sacramento, CA: California Department of Education Press.

Trentacosta, C. J., & Izard, C. E. (2007). Kindergarten children's emotion competence as a predictor of their academic competence in first grade. *Emotion, 7*, 77–88.

True Cost. (2009). *List of countries with universal healthcare*. Retrieved from http://truecostblog.com/2009/08/09/countries-with-universal-healthcare-by-date/

U.S. Census Bureau. (2011). Maternity leave and employment patterns of first-time mothers: 1961–2008. Washington, DC: Author.

U.S. Congress. (1984). Report of Select Committee on Children, Youth, and Families. Washington, DC: Author.

U.S. Department of Health and Human Services. (2011a). *Executive summary: The Surgeon General's call to action to support breastfeeding*. Washington, DC: Author.

U.S. Department of Health and Human Services. (2011b). *News release: Everyone can help make breastfeeding easier, Surgeon General says in "call to action."* Retrieved from http://www.hhs.gov/news/press/2011pres/01/20110120a.html

U.S. Department of Health and Human Services. (2011c). *Routine prenatal care*. Retrieved from http://guideline.gov/content.aspx?id=24138#Section420

U.S. Department of Labor. (2007). *Women in the labor force: A databook (2007 edition)*. Retrieved from http://www.bls.gov/cps/wlf-databook2007.htm

U.S. Department of Labor. (2009). *Labor force participation of women and mothers: 2008*. Retrieved from http://www.bls.gov/opub/ted/2009/ted_20091009.htm

U.S. Food and Drug Administration. (1996). Food labeling: Health claims and label statements; folate and neural tube defects. Federal Register 61 FR 8752 (Vol. 61).

U.S. Preventive Services Task Force. (2009). Screening for depression in adults: U.S. Preventive Services Task Force recommendation statement. *Annals of Internal Medicine, 151*(11), 784–792.

U.S. Public Health Service. (2000). *Treating tobacco use and dependence: A systems approach*. Rockville, MD: Office of the U.S. Surgeon General; U.S. Public Health Service; U.S. Department of Health and Human Services.

Van der Zee, B., de Beaufort, I., Temel, S., de Wert, G., Denktas, S., & Steegers, E. (2011). Preconception care: An essential preventive strategy to improve children's and women's health. *Journal of Public Health Policy, 32*, 367–379.

Vaughn, B. E., Kopp, C. B., & Krakow, J. B. (1984). The emergence and consolidation of self-control from eighteen to thirty months of age: Normative trends and individual differences. *Child Development, 55*(3), 990–1004.

Ventura, S. J., Martin, J. A., Curtin, S. C., & Mathews, T. J. (1997). Report of final natality statistics, 1995. *Monthly Vital Statistics Report, 45*(11).

Waldfogel, J. (1999). The impact of the Family and Medical Leave Act. *Journal of Policy Analysis and Management, 18*(2), 281–302.

Walker, D. C., McCully, L., & Vest, V. (2001). Evidence-based prenatal care visits: When less is more. *Journal of Midwifery & Women's* Health, *46*, 146–151.

Washbrook, E., Ruhm, C. J., Waldfogel, J., & Han, W.-J. (2011). Public policies, women's employment after childbearing, and child well-being. *The B.E. Journal of Economic Analysis & Policy, 11*(1), 43.

Weinberg, M. K., & Tronick, E. Z. (1998). Emotional characteristics of infants associated with maternal depression and anxiety. *Pediatrics, 102*(5), 1298–1304.

Weir, K. (2012). The beginnings of mental illness. *Monitor on Psychology, 43*(2), 36.

Weiss, R. E. (2012). *Pregnancy & childbirth: Readers respond—When did you get to see your midwife or doctor?* Retrieved from http://pregnancy.about.com/u/ua/prenatalcare/firstprenatalvisit.htm

Whitebook, M., & Bellm, D. (1999). *Taking on turnover.* Washington, DC: Center for the Child Care Workforce.

Whitebook, M., Howes, C., & Phillips, D. (1990). *Who cares? Child care teachers and the quality of care in America. Final report: National Child Care Staffing Study.* Oakland, CA: Child Care Employee Project.

Winegarden, C. R., & Bracy, P. (1995). Demographic consequences of maternal-leave programs in industrial countries: Evidence from fixed effects models. *Southern Economic Journal, 61,* 1020–1035.

World Health Organization. (2012). *Nutrition: Exclusive breastfeeding.* Retrieved from http://www.who.int/nutrition/topics/exclusive_breastfeeding/en/

Yazejian, N., & Bryant, D. M. (2010). *Promising early returns: Educare implementation study data.* Chapel Hill, NC: Frank Porter Graham Child Development Institute.

Zahn-Waxler, C., & Radke-Yarrow, M. (1990). The origins of empathetic concern. *Motivation and Emotion, 14,* 107–130.

ZERO TO THREE. (2007). The infant-toddler set-aside of the Child Care and Development Block Grant: Improving quality child care for infants and toddlers. Washington, DC: ZERO TO THREE Policy Center.

Zhou, F., Santoli, J., Messonnier, M. L., Yusuf, H. R., Shefer, A., Chu, S. Y., Rodewald, L., & Harpaz, R. (2005). Economic evaluation of the 7-vaccine routine childhood immunization schedule in the United States, 2001. *Archives of Pediatrics & Adolescent Medicine, 159*(2), 1136–1144.

Zigler, E. F., Marsland, K., & Lord, H. (2009). *The tragedy of child care in America.* New Haven, CT: Yale University Press.

Index

The letter *f* following a page number refers to a figure.

About the Author

J. Ronald Lally, EdD, is one of the pioneers in the field of infant/toddler development. In 1968 he received his doctorate in educational psychology with a focus on infancy from the University of Florida and a postdoctoral certificate for infant testing from the Child Development Research Centre in London. While at Florida, he directed one of the first home-visiting programs for infants in the United States. For many years he was a professor at Syracuse University and chair of its Department of Child and Family Studies. There he ran the Syracuse University Family Development Research Program, a longitudinal study of the impact of early intervention on children from low-income families. Part of that study was the operation of the Syracuse University Children's Center, the first federally funded infant care center in the country. Currently he is the co-director of the Center for Child and Family Studies at WestEd, a research, development, and service agency based in San Francisco where, for the past 27 years, he has directed the work of its Program for Infant/Toddler Care.

Dr. Lally consults nationally and internationally on programs and policies for infants, toddlers, and their families. He has produced 20 videos on quality infant/toddler care that are used worldwide. He is one of the founders of ZERO TO THREE: National Center for Infants, Toddlers, and Families and served on the Health and Human Services Advisory Committee that developed the national initiative Early Head Start.

Some of his recent publications include "Want Success in Schools? Start with Babies!," in *Kappa Delta Pi Record, Vol. 48,* (2012); "The Link Between Consistent Caring Interactions with Babies, Early Brain Development, and School Readiness," in *The Pre-K Debates: Current Controversies and Issues* (Zigler, Gilliam, & Barnett, Eds., Brookes Publishing, 2011); "Chapter Two: The Program for Infant Toddler Care," in *Approaches to Early Childhood Education* (6th ed., Roopnarine & Johnson, Eds., Pearson, 2011); and "School Readiness Begins in Infancy: Social Interactions During the First Two Years of Life Provide the Foundation for Learning," in *Kappan Magazine* (November 2010).

FOR OUR BABIES
A CALL FOR BETTER BEGINNINGS

For additional resources related to this book's content and information about how you can participate in the For Our Babies movement, please visit www.forourbabies.org.

DATE DUE